GREENER P.
THE GERALD PIERCE STORY

A LIFE'S COLLECTION OF STORIES ABOUT FARMING WITH HORSES AND EARLY TRACTORS

AS TOLD TO HERBERT SACK

Copyright © 2022 by Herbert Sack. All Rights Reserved.

No part of this publication may be reproduced, distributed, or transmitted in any form or by any means, including photocopying, recording, or other electronic or mechanical methods, or by any information storage and retrieval system without the prior written permission of the publisher, except in the case of very brief quotations embodied in critical reviews and certain other noncommercial uses permitted by copyright law.

This book was published thanks to free support and training from:

TCKPublishing.com

CONTENTS

Why I Wrote This Book 2

What You Will Find in This Book 3

Chapter 1. Starting out in Colorado 4

Chapter 2. The Road to Oregon 15

Chapter 3. Home to Nebraska 28

Chapter 4. Spring of 1924 41

Chapter 5. Iowa Days 66

Chapter 6. Return to Nebraska 82

Chapter 7. On My Own and Partnering Up 99

About The Author 120

Other Works By Herbert Sack 121

Why I Wrote This Book

Anyone who knew my Uncle Gerald, at least later in his life, knew that he loved to tell stories about the past. He enjoyed recounting events from his life with attention to details as if they had happened just last week. He was a wealth of knowledge on how things used to be done.

When Gerald was getting on in years I started meeting with him in the evenings and on weekends in an effort to record some of his stories, while he was still alive to tell them. There were many stories that took place after he left the farm and went to work on the ag campus at the University of Nebraska; this book focuses on the stories from his birth to his last days of farming.

What You Will Find in This Book.

The stories that make up this book are a historical recollection of how life on the farm was during the transition from farming with horses to the use of early tractors. It tells what farm families had to do to survive through difficult times. The history in this book's pages explains how things were done in the early 20th century. Whether you knew Gerald or not his historical account of things like bailing hay before modern hay bailers and driving Model T touring cars over mountain passes provide history in an entertaining setting.

Starting Out in Colorado

I was born in the hospital at Lamar, Colorado, a small two-bit town just west of the Kansas border. The fact that I was born in the hospital wouldn't be so all fired important, except that it was 1911. In those days if you lived out on the farm, or in most cases even in town, you were probably born in the same bed you were conceived in. If a woman was lucky there'd be a midwife or a neighbor lady around. It wasn't unusual for a woman to have to tough it out alone on the prairie. I don't know if it was my mom's or my dad's idea that they should travel to the hospital. I'm pretty sure though that they were both in agreement that they ought to do it. Maybe they were both scared of what might happen. I can tell you for certain why I was born in the hospital.

My Dad, Walter Pierce, married a farm girl named Liddia Taggert. She grew up on a place a couple of miles west of Waverly, Nebraska. Not too far from where my dad grew up. I think they got married about three years before I was born. Not too long after they got married, they took off to set up housekeeping in Eastern Colorado. Land was cheap there, and if a man worked hard, they said a pretty good life could be had. They hadn't been married a full year when Liddia went into labor. She gave birth to a baby boy. It wasn't the happy time it should have been for them though. Something had gone wrong when the baby came. It wasn't a clean birth or something. Liddia died the next week. The baby died three days after her. The baby just couldn't make it without his mother's milk. It was a pretty bad time for Dad. Liddia and the baby were put on the train and were buried back in Nebraska.

I can't say exactly why, whether it was out of love for Liddia, grief, desperation, or exactly what brought Dad to do what he did next, but not too long after the funeral Dad married my mom, Laura. She was Liddia's younger sister. So that's why when it came time for Mom to deliver me, my dad hitched up the horse and buggy and drove the twelve miles up the road to the hospital at Lamar.

Our farm was just outside of Bristol, Colorado. It was a rundown homestead that Dad had been able to buy reasonably. He was trying to fix it up as he could. Bristol was in about the same shape. It was small even for a small town. There weren't much more than a few houses clustered around a few scattered businesses. You could say it looked a bit like birds huddled together against a winter storm. The dirt streets turned to ankle-deep mud when it rained and became choked with dust when it didn't. Most of the time it didn't. In the dry summer, you could get dirty just walking across the street. I guess you could call it a street being it was a town, but it weren't nothing but a dirty path between the houses where the grass had worn away. There sure wasn't any hospital to be found there.

With all this in mind when Mom was getting close to when she thought she ought to be ready to deliver, she and Dad drove the buggy up the road that wound alongside the Arkansas River to Lamar. The rough ride must have done some good to get me into position because I was born without a problem. Things went well enough with my birth that the rest of my brothers and sisters who came along after me found their way into the world in the old feather bed at home.

I don't remember all that much about those early days in Colorado, but I do remember going to church. Going to church was one of the most important things that happened. Out on the farm, you worked hard from sunup to sundown. And unless you were trading work with somebody there wasn't much of a chance to see anybody except on Sunday. It may not have been as important what the preacher said in his sermon as it was what all got talked about afterward. For a pretty good spell after church everyone just sort of stayed put, a little reluctant to go back to what was waiting them. They talked about everything that needed talked about. Who was sick or had died. Who'd lost a cow or was going to get married. Who was doing what they ought to be doing and more importantly who wasn't. They talked about it all. The women never really got clear out of the church. They just congregated by the front steps while the men went out to check on the horses. Checking on the horses was an excuse to get far enough out of earshot of the pastor they could be a bit coarser with their speech and they could have a smoke or a chew. The horses were doing just fine. They just needed that distance and with it a bit more freedom out away from the women and the preacher. The preacher never made it out as far as the horses. The women usually kept him busy.

Everybody seemed to know their place. For us kids, it was out back. It was the only time we had to play with other kids, and we weren't about to waste any time standing around talking. We tore around like a band of bangies until somebody's Dad yelled out that they were going. Once that happened it spread like a disease. It wouldn't be too long before we were all packed up and headed down the road for home.

You never had to drive a horse home. They knew when they were going home and moved along a little faster to get back to the barn. Even after a long hard day in the field when you headed back home you could hardly home them back. Especially once they came in sight of the barn, that made em half crazy. If you let em have the reigns they'd break into a run.

Maybe because going to church was so important, or maybe it was just because we did it so often, but that's where my first memory starts. I must have been almost four years old. My little sister Olive would have been two then. She was sitting in the seat between my Mom and Dad. Mom was holding my little brother Charlie. He was still just a baby. I had a little box on the floorboards that I sat on. Dad had nailed it together out of some old barn boards, so I'd have something to sit on. It made me just tall enough that I could see the mares' back over the buckboard. While we drove along. I watched Dad drive the mares, pretending that I was the one doing the driving. I'd call out commands repeating what he had just said and then watch as the horses responded pretending that it was me, they were listening to. I even tied on couple of pieces of strap leather to the dashboard to use as pretend reigns when we went somewhere. That's what I have for my first memory was pretending that I was driving the team to church.

My grandpa lived with us then. but don't remember him ever going anywhere with us. He didn't leave the farm much then. He had always been as tough as an old hedge post, and now in his seventies, he was starting to look as weathered as one. Dad said he used to be tall and strong when he was a young man. He still seemed plenty tall enough to me. I remember his finger especially. He lost it when he was a young man. He left his home in Ohio and ran off during the Civil War to join up with the Wisconsin regiment. When he finally came back to Ohio, he was missing a finger. It had been shot off by a mini ball. He was lucky that a finger was all he had lost. After the war, he didn't stay around Ohio any longer than to marry Grandma. They struck out to make their fortune in a place he'd heard talked about during the war, Nebraska. It was open for settlers, and a great many were striking out for the land of the flat waters, as the Indians called it.

The two of them staked out a claim on a homestead just outside of Weeping Water. Where they stayed for a few years till Grandpa got the notion that they could find a better place. They moved around eastern Nebraska staying on one farm or another just long enough for Grandpa to decide that corn was growing better in another county and off they went again. They moved less often the older they got. They had stayed put on a on a farm west of Waverly for a pretty good spell and when Grandma died that put an end to the moving around. At least till Grandpa decided to retire.

By the time Mom and Dad got married Grandpa had already spent too much time in one spot. He pulled up stakes leaving the farm to his daughter and her husband and went off to live with my Mom and Dad in Colorado. Grandpa had never put down any deep roots or rode out any bad times. When things got bad he pulled up stakes and moved on looking for a better life. Whether he found that better life in Colorado or not it was his last stop. He went up to bed one cold winter night and never came down for breakfast. The train took him back to Nebraska where he was laid to rest next to Grandma in the family plot.

Southeastern Colorado was as dry as the buffalo bones that lay bleaching in the sun while the dry Colorado winds slowly turned them back to dust. It was ranch country and should have stayed that way. The only thing it was good for was running cattle or sheep on the grasslands, but alongside the Arkansas River, there was a system of canals that had been dug to carry irrigation water out onto the dry parched prairie where a handful of farmers tried to convince the land to produce a meager crop. The main canal was a big trench that had been dug by hand. The men who dug it threw the dirt up along the side as they went. From a distance, it looked like a giant mole had crawled through the prairie. Coming off the main run were the floodgates that fed water to five or six farms. The dry ground soaked up water like a sponge. There just wasn't enough water in the canal to feed all the farms so the gates were opened one at a time. You had to wait your turn for water. There wasn't any particular schedule for when the gates would be opened either. You never knew when the rider would be coming through saying the water was coming. When it did though whether it was daylight or two in the morning you had to go work the water into the fields while it was coming down the chute.

The only thing that such sporadic watering was any good for was growing a hay crop. Harvesting the hay wasn't any easier than trying to keep it irrigated. We had a horse drawn mower with two big iron-lugged wheels.

The wheels drove the gearbox that ran the cycle bar. This all hung off the right side of the mower so all day long you made clockwise turns around the fields. The tongue and the iron seat bolted right to the axle so every bump every hole the mower hit shot right up threw the seat. The hay fields were big enough that by the time you were done cutting, you could start raking what you had cut earlier into windrows. Everybody that did any amount of haying had a dump rake. That was all there was. The first side delivery rake didn't come along for another twenty years. The dump rake had two big old iron wheels and a row of spring metal teeth that hooked into the back. The team drove the rake across the field gathering hay and every time you came to a windrow you pulled the trip lever dumping the rake. Then you stepped on the pedal and the rake dropped back down and rolled the trip lever back into place. You had to be careful when that lever rolled back forward so that it didn't catch you. If it did it could throw you forward off the rake and end up being drug around under the rake.

If it didn't rain, and it rarely did, you could put the hay up in five days. The only thing you could do with that much hay was to try and sell it. If you were going to sell hay the only buyer was the army. It had to be bailed because you had to haul it down to the rail yard and ship it out by train. Dad was the only one of the neighbors who had bought a hay bailer What we had back then, and for a good many years to come was a stationary bailer. You didn't parade it up and down the field. It stayed put and you bucked the hay into it. The bailer ran off of a horsepower. That was a big iron gear with cogs on the inside that drove three planetary gears. This all was turned by a team of horses walking a beam in a circle. The planetary gears reduced the drive down and fed power to an iron shaft called the tumbling rod. It came out the bottom of the horsepower and could be hooked up to whatever you needed to have it drive. In this case, it was the Jackshaft on the bailer that drove the plunge rod down to pack the hay into bails. It just kept rotating up and down driving the hay tighter and tighter until you had enough packed into the machine to tie off a bail.

You brought the hay in from the windrows with a hay buck. It was a skid with two big wheels in the front about fourteen feet apart. In between the wheels were wooden tangs that picked up the windrow as you drug it down the field. A horse was tied to a single tree outside each wheel so there had to be a separate set of reigns running to each horse. The only way to turn the buck was to drive one horse and hold the other one back. When the buck was full it was driven back so it could be forked into the bailer. Making bails was all a matter of timing. When you forked the hay into the bailer you had to pay attention to the timing of the plunge rod. Otherwise, it would come down and catch your fork and drive it inside the bailer.

By the time Grandpa died Dad had already had his fill of night irrigating and the speculative hay market. Canal irrigating and taking the water whenever you could get it seemed to be the only future there was going to be in eastern Colorado. Dad did what Grandpa had taught him best. He called up the auctioneer and put the farm up for sale. There had to be a better place to make a living than this.

Farm sales were as much a happening as if the circus had come to town. Almost as important as the chance to pick up a secondhand implement was the opportunity to stand around swapping stories chewing horseshoe brand plug tobacco or smoking hand-rolled cigarettes with the other farmers. I've seen cigarettes that were rolled by farmers pinching the paper with a couple of fingers while filling it from the pouch that after a quick trip across the tongue looked every bit as well made as if it had come out of a box. If a fellow had good teeth, you could bite off a piece of the hard plug tobacco, like tearing off jerky. Most of the older men carried a jack knife so they could whittle off a chunk. If you passed a plug to a fellow standing next to you, you passed the knife along with it. The sale wasn't at all like after church. Nobody cared about how you went about saying what you said or how you were acting. It was just a day for unrestrained socializing.

I don't remember whether it was the neighbor ladies who did it or if it was the women from the church but back then everybody that came to the sale got a sack lunch and a cup of coffee. It was just the way things were done back then because whether you were working for hire on a thrashing crew or just swapping labor with one of the neighbors you always got your lunch where you were working. Usually, the women worked every bit as hard cooking meals as the men did in the fields. I know my mom did. She started early in the morning baking bread. Pies had to be baked and the potatoes boiled. There was always a roast to be put in the oven and the table to be set. Then she cleaned it all up and started again.

The sale day was like a day at the state fair. Nobody worked in the field on the day of the sale. You got up early enough to lay out some feed for the livestock and hitch up the team. After that, you were off for the day. It was as much a holiday as if it had been declared so by law.

The days after the sale took place the little white farmhouse looked a bit abandoned. All the livestock and the farm machinery were gone. It was late spring, and the grass hadn't been cut for a while. It was pretty quiet with everything gone except for a couple of laying hens. What had been my first home would soon be behind me and it probably would have been a bit sad except for the excitement of the trip we were about to take.

The Road to Oregon.

I remember running around the yard getting all worked up while Mom and Dad finished tying what little we had left onto a homemade trailer. Dad had built it out of an old buggy frame and had made a hitch so it could be hitched onto the back of the Model T Ford touring car we had bought with some of the hay money last year. It was an open touring car with canvas flaps that you dropped down when it was raining or if it was cold out. The flaps had icing glass sown into them, but it was easily cracked or broken with the winter wind. Dad had taken them off and took them into town to have the harness man sew new ones into them. I couldn't wait for it to rain so we could put them down. For me just having new icing glass was like having a whole new car.

When everything was on the trailer or shoved into the back, where my brother and I were going to sit, Dad set the throttle lever and retarded the spark on the motor. Next, he put a block under the front wheel walked around to the front, and cranked the motor over. Once he was satisfied that it was running good and wasn't going to sputter out and die, he pulled the block out from under the front wheel. The Model T started to shake its way forward as if to give him the signal that it was time to jump into the seat and start off. They were an impatient breed of cars. The old Model Ts ran from a set of bands. As soon as the motor fired up it started to pull against those bands. I heard stories of people getting pinned or even crushed against the front wall of their garage when they forgot to block the wheels before they cranked one of them over.

Dad pushed down on the forward pedal, and we jerked back in our seats as the motor stained into its burden. Pushing down on the forward pedal puts you into low. It didn't go very fast, but you had all the power that you needed. Then as he let it back out it slipped over into high range, and we headed down the lane toward the road. What was a road back then wasn't what a road is now. What once were wagon trails and cart paths had been graded out and small ditches cut along the sides. Now a few cars shared the roads with the horses and mules that pulled the freight to where the trains didn't yet go. I don't remember as much about living in Colorado as I do about leaving it. We were headed out on the road bound for who knows where. I suppose that Dad knew sort of where he was going but even if he had told me, it wouldn't have meant anything because the only place, I'd ever known was Colorado. I hadn't even been to school yet to have heard about the places we were about to go through. Driving down the farm road for the last time didn't seem as important then as it does now as I look back on it, but it changed everything for me.

On the farm next to ours lived a boy that I had played with every time that I had the chance to. I can't recall his name right now, but I know that I never saw him again. I did hear of him more though because years later we heard on the radio that he had made the first mail flight from Omaha to Cheyenne. Back then we'd never seen anything but a few old biplanes so that was still pretty big news. I waved goodbye as we passed their place. A couple of miles down the road we turned down the lane that would take us to Champ Meyer's place. Champ was a bit younger than Dad, but they had gotten off real well right from the start. It was like they'd grown up and gone to school together and knew each other for a long time and not just the few short years that they had. Champ was a little bit bigger than my dad and with me being a little boy he seemed every bit as strong as a mule. One day I'd seen him walk over to where two grown men were trying to throw a heavy iron plow into a wagon box. Champ motioned them aside and threw it up into the wagon like it weren't no more than a sack of feed.

Champ and Dad were always trading work at each other's place. It seemed like he was always over to our place, or we were over to his. For some reason, Champ and Dad weren't going to say goodbye just like that. Champ had decided that they were going to go along and see where we ended up. The farm work was all done for the year so all that was needed was to throw feed to the livestock Champ had gotten old Charlie Grew to look after his place while they were gone. Charlie had quit school after the third grade. I'd never seen him in church, and I never saw him wear anything besides a pair of bib overalls that had been patched so many times that he looked like a rodeo clown. He looked even more like a clown cause he always had a chunk of plug tobacco the size of a walnut making his cheek stick out. He'd been a hired hand all his life. He never took him no wife nor even tried to rent a farm of his own. Charlie was the kind of guy that needed to work for somebody else. He needed to be told what to do or he wouldn't do anything. Soon as you told him though he'd work as hard as anybody.

When we turned into their lane, I could see that their car was all loaded up and ready to go. They were sitting on the front porch drinking tea out of mason jars. It was mostly just well water sweetened with molasses. There were a few handshakes with old Charlie and we were all packed back in the car ready to hit the road.

We spent the next seven weeks camping out in an old white canvas tent. We were headed for nowhere in particular and not in much hurry to get there. We started out on the old south highway headed for the Rockies and the Great Divide. South not so much because it went south but because it took you to the south pass over the Rocky Mountains. It was better crossing, or so most people said.

Greener Pastures

The old Model T Fords were about as simple of a car as was ever built. It didn't have any water pump and it didn't have a fuel pump. Hot water rose to the top of the radiator and sank to the bottom as it cooled. because there wasn't any pressure you could plug a leak with just about anything. Oatmeal was good because it swelled up and held tight. The gas tank was right under the front seat. Just high enough above the engine so as to let the gas run downhill into the carburetor by gravity. If you went up a steep grade that was any length at all the gas wouldn't reach the carburetor and when the engine used up all the gas that was in the settling bowl it would stall out. The mountain roads were too long and steep. They'd never been cut down and the road was just as steep as the mountain you were climbing. What you had to do to climb a mountain road was to turn the car around and go up the hill in reverse. That way it put the gas tank up above the motor again and the gas would run into the carburetor.

Before going up the divide we had to stop the car and tie the trailer onto the front bumper of the Model T. When we thought we were ready we started off backing up the mountain. Dad had his foot on the reverse pedal and leaned out the side of the car so he could see where he was going. The car was too full of stuff to turn around to be able to see so he had to lean out the window to keep from running off the winding road. A little over halfway up the divide, I got tired of trying to see where we were

19

headed and turned back around in the seat and looked at where we had come from. We were high enough up that we could see for further than I had ever been able to see before. Mom was pointing things out for us to try and see. Dad never saw it happen, but he heard Mom and I scream. The trailer came loose from where it had been tied to the front bumper and started down the mountainside. There was nothing we could do but watch it take off faster and faster down the road. At the first curve, it went off the edge and down into a ravine spilling boxes and suitcases all over the hillside. Dad let the Model T roll back down the hill to where the trailer had disappeared over the edge and set the hand brake. The trailer had hit some trees and stopped just a little ways from the road but the rest of the stuff kept going. We spent half the day picking up things and putting them back into the boxes so it could be carried back up the hillside. Dad and Champ tied a lasso onto the trailer and pulled it back up the hill using the car. I thought about that day many times for years to come. Every time we took to traveling and went to get out the suitcases, I thought about it because there were suitcases with battered up sides around the house till We started moving out on our own.

With the trailer securely tied to the front of the bumper we made it over the divide and headed southwest toward New Mexico and Arizona. We went by the Painted Desert and the Grand Canyon, that was one hell of a big hole in the ground. At the Navajo Indian reservation, we bought a couple of handmade Navajo rugs. Those were well-made rugs because they laid on the wooden floors of the houses that we lived in for the next twenty-five years.

Just south of Los Angeles at the port of San Pedro, we left the cars behind and got on the ferry that went out to Catalina Island. We stayed around Orange County for almost a week, but Dad decided that Southern California wasn't right for us, so we headed up north to Oregon. Dad eventually put money down on a farm about ninety miles south of Portland. On the farm, there was a small brownish-orange brick house with a small garage made out of pine car siding. There was a barn that was really more the size of a good-sized tool shed. This was apple country, and every farm had a good-sized orchard of apples and peaches. The Calapooya river cut right through the middle of the farm. On the same side of the river where the house was built were the orchards. There was a good stand of timber on either side of the river and beyond that there was a patch of about forty acres that could be farmed. We had a little rowboat that we kept tied to the bank for if you needed to get across quick. To do farming though we had to drive the team down the road to the covered bridge to cross over.

As dry as Eastern Colorado was Oregon was about as wet as it gets. It rained for nine months out of the year. Dad had grown up in corn country and it seemed right to him to bust up the tillable soil and lay corn into the furrows. It rained so much in the spring that the seed corn just rotted in the ground. Dad replanted it four times that first year. Finally, he gave up and bought what's called a trip line lister. It was a strange tool to use. A wire had to be stretched across the field and every forty-two inches you tied a knot in the wire. The lister had to be fed through the wire and as the horses pulled it across the field every time it came to a knot it dropped three or four seeds into a hill. In these little hills finally, the corn came up and could grow. It didn't make good corn though. It rained too much, and it just never produced like it ought to have. We pretty much had to count on the apples and peaches to pay the bank and to have money to live on. There never seemed to be enough money to do either. Every year we had to borrow money against next year's crop to live on.

In the fall when the apples and peaches were ripe, everybody picked fruit. Most of the farmers stored them in boxes until December when the prices started to come up a little bit before selling. Just about every farm building that had a little space was stuffed with apple boxes. Even the Garages were lined with apples leaving just enough room to get the car in and out of.

Apples were hard to make a living on. If you had a good crop, then the prices were low. If you didn't have any to sell, then the price was respectable. Three years after we moved to Oregon it happened. Something that never happens in that part of Oregon in December. It froze. All the apples were ruined and with it the cash crop for the year.

We didn't have anything to pay the banknote with. There wasn't anything to be done. The bank would be taking over the farm, so before they came and moved us off, we moved to Albany Oregon. Dad found a job working on a construction crew. It wasn't much money but he managed to put a little bit aside. We stayed there just long enough to save up train fare back to Nebraska, where Mom and Dad were from.

The train ride is still pretty clear to me. The passenger cars weren't nothing like they are now. They weren't nothing but a box car whose windows had been cut in with wooden benches to sit on. At night we slept on the benches or on the floor between them. It weren't no picnic, although that's how we ate. There wasn't any food other than the food and sandwiches that Mom had packed. We drank water out of a canteen and watched the train wind its way through the mountains in Wyoming and cross the rolling prairies of western Nebraska. The old coal-fired trains may seem romantic as you look back on them, but boy they were filthy. The dirty soot from the smokestack drifted in the windows and everything had a layer of grim on it. When they finally started converting the coal-burning locomotives over to burning diesel, I don't think there was anybody sorry to see the change.

Greener Pastures

Mom kept telling me not to stick my head out the window because of the blowing cinders. She kept saying "You're going to get a cinder in your eye. It was a long trip though, and eventually, she gave up scolding me. Probably it was because she had told me not to, I had my head out the window watching the heavy black smoke belching out of the smokestack. I jerked back inside screaming and crying. Mom knew just what had happened. I don't know how she did it with me screaming and kicking from the pain, but she got me down on a bench and got the cinder out with her handkerchief. It was one of those magicians' handkerchiefs that seemed to appear from out of nowhere when she needed it. She worked the cinder out and saved my eye. I was a little better behaved for the rest of the train ride.

What had been three days on the train seemed more like it had been three weeks. By the time the train began to slow for the station at Alliance, we had all learned to brace ourselves for the jolt that was about to come. To stop the train in the right place on the platform the engineer put the big iron wheels in reverse, spinning them slightly, to stop the train. The cars banged against their couplings as the slack went out of them and the train came to a stop. If you weren't ready the train would throw you out of your seat onto the floor.

It was early morning when the train came into town. The town was just starting to wake up. The three of us kids were so full of energy from being cooped up on the train for so long that we ran up and down the thick wooden planked dock making noise like a cattle stampede. We had to wait for the two-yard hands to unload our boxes and what farm implements Dad had kept. By the time they had our belongings piled up on the platform the morning sun had come up and things were starting to move around town. We left everything we owned sitting on the platform and never gave it a second thought while we walked over to the main street to find a cafe. We had to wait until late afternoon when the southbound train that would take us down to Gurley would come through. We had the whole day to spend in town. My mother's brother lived about sixty miles south in a little town called Gurley, Nebraska.

Not too far from the station, we found a cafe. It was a red brick building with a sloped flat roof. The front of the building rose up a good five feet higher than the rest of the walls. It made the building look taller than it was. The smell of breakfast and fresh rolls poured through the wooden screen door in the front letting you know it was a good place to eat before you even got there. It was good to smell something besides the heavy smell of burnt coal. Inside the cafe, we sat on the first chairs that weren't hard wooden benches and weren't moving since we left Oregon. The big wooden cookstove in the back made it uncomfortably warm even in the coolness of the morning. There was a hand-lettered signboard on the back wall with the menu and prices. We sat down at one of the tables that were a collection of mismatched kitchen tables and chairs that had been accumulated through the years. Once we were settled in the cook came out from behind the short wooden walls that separated off the kitchen from the tables to bring us coffee and take our orders. I don't know if the breakfast was really that good or if it was the three days of eating sandwiches on the train, but I still think that those were the best biscuits and gravy I've ever had.

There wasn't much to do after breakfast, so we walked down to the park to wait until the southbound came through. It sure felt good to be off the train for a while. There was a hand pump in the park and we washed as much of the smell of burnt coal off of us as we could with the cool well water. A couple of hours rest in the park had been just what we needed before getting back on the train. We played around there, and I found a pocket knife that I still have. I had hit the jackpot. I showed it to everybody for the next couple of days.

The ride down to Gurley was only two hours long. It went by pretty fast compared to what we had already been through. The train only stopped once. That was at Bridgeport, right after we crossed over the Platte River. Every time the train stopped, we got off. No matter how short the stop was. And we didn't get back on till the conductor hollered out the "all aboard". While we were still at the station my Dad went into the office and sent

Greener Pastures

a wire down to my uncle to let him know we would be arriving today. That way they would be waiting for us when the train pulled into the station in Gurley.

Home to Nebraska

My uncle ran the grain elevator in Gurley. It was hard work when the harvest was going on. There were a lot of wagons lined up that had to be unloaded. Most of the year though he was able to set his own schedule. Besides if anybody needed to buy some chicken feed or something and he wasn't in, they'd just come over to the house. I ignored the cinders and stuck my head out the window as the train rolled into the station. I could see them all there standing on the platform waiting for the train to squeal to a stop. I knew it was them. Not because they were the only ones standing on the platform but because they looked just like I had imagined they would from their letters. My Mom and Uncle had always written letters back and forth. When they came Mom would read them to us after dinner with all the excitement of a well-written book. I had a pretty good picture in my mind just from those letters.

We stayed at Gurley for a couple of weeks. We hadn't planned on staying long but we knew it would be a while before we'd see my uncle again. My Dad and uncle loaded the boxes into one of my uncle's wagons and we drug them over to the train platform again where we said our goodbyes and took the train to Sidney. At Sidney, we caught an eastbound train, on to Lincoln, where Dad's sister lived. The tracks followed the Platte run along the old Oregon Trail. There are a lot of towns that sprung up along the old trail and the train stopped at every one of them. seemed like we'd just get a good head of steam built up and the engineer would start blowing off to slow down for the next town. Even though the trip took longer because of all the stops we didn't seem to get so bored just knowing we were getting closer to what Mom and Dad called home.

My folks had left Lincoln ten years earlier when they headed for Colorado. We moved in with my mother's brother Luther Tager, who I had never heard called anything except Uncle Lou. He and his wife Pearl lived in a house at University Place, a small town just a few miles east of Lincoln. My grandpa Tager was staying there, and I remember my brother and I slept with him just like we had when he came to visit us in Oregon. Ever since Grandma died Grandpa had been visiting. He was retired and moved from one of his kids to the next. Both of my grandmothers died before I met them and Grandpa Pierce died when I was so young I don't remember him well. Grandpa Tager was the only grandparent who got the chance to really spoil me like grandparents are supposed to.

We didn't just come into town without a plan. Before we left Oregon, we had gotten a letter from my aunt Pearl, who used to be Pearl Schnider, that the James Schnider farm north of Waverly was going to be without a renter in the fall. James Schnider had bought a farm down in Kansas and was moving his family from his place on the Salt Creek. Pearl and Luther had arranged for us to take it over. They were going to stay on the farm through the winter and move down to Kansas as soon as the spring thaw came. I can't say that I blame him for wanting to move. Before the Corp of Engineers came through and straightened the creek out it wound around cutting right through the place cutting it in half. Between the timber on both sides and the creek there wasn't but about seventy acres out of one hundred and sixty that was farmable.

My uncle Lou wasn't a farmer at all. He worked as the state bank examiner. He had a mind for numbers. I have seen him run down a column of numbers with his pencil and just like that put the total down at the end. He was faster than any machine was back then. He worked for the state until 1929 when he took a job as a cashier at the Lancaster State Bank in Waverly. He had a pretty good-sized house in University Place. Even though it was a big house with two kids of his own and what with Grandpa and us staying there it became crowded. It was obvious we couldn't stay there till the Schniders moved off their place. Not to mention that Dad was one that needed to be doing something. Around Uncle Lou's house in town, there wasn't much that needed to be done. Dad finally came across the Walker boys who were in need of someone to move into their tenant house and help them pick corn that fall. Mom and Dad had known the Walker boys since back in high school.

Even though they were grown men everybody still called them the Walker boys. That seems to happen with a couple of bachelors. Mom said that when they were younger, they were both dating a girl and were thinking serious about her till they found out that each one of them was seeing the same girl. She ran off and got married to Roy Copple. After that, neither one of them ever dated again.

The Walker boys had an old maid cousin who was working as a lady's maid over in England. They wrote her a few letters and convinced her to come back over and keep house for them. With their cousin around to look after them they could spend all their time looking after their farms or buying another one. They eventually acquired quite a bit of land. They also needed quite a bit of help to farm it all. We moved into their tenant house and Dad went to picking corn for the Walker boys.

My sister Olive and I rode the school bus into Waverly that fall to start school. We went to the old one-room schoolhouse where they taught the third and fourth grades together. It stood right where the DL&D cut the town into a triangle. The rest of the kids went over to the two-story church building up the road. The school bus that hauled us to town wasn't nothing more than a truck with a roof overhead. There were two long benches, one running down each side. It held about ten kids if they weren't too big. Along the roof on each side was a canvas curtain that could be dropped down and snapped at the bottom to keep the cold wind out in the winter. It wasn't much better than being out in the open. It seemed like most of the time if it wasn't frozen it was mud. It rained in the spring and fall and with the rain came the mud. The school bus had a Ruxell Rocky Mountain rear end. Once we got onto the gravel highway the driver could kick it over into high and we could scoot down the road at thirty-five miles an hour. At that time what's now called Highway #6 was the old DL&D, which was short for Detroit, Lincoln, and Denver. It was the only gravel road in the county. Everything else was dirt. Whenever it rained, once we turned off the highway, we spent the rest of the way home in low axle churning axle-deep mud. It was so noisy in the back from the rear end and wheels churning mud that you couldn't hear yourself think. If it was really bad when we got to the corner that was a mile south and a mile west of town the driver would make us all get out and we'd stand there and wait while he plowed the mud three-quarters of a mile down and back to let the Dietrick girl off at her place. Then when he would come back from dropping her off, we'd pile back in and continue down the road.

In the spring of 1922, we moved from the Walker Boys tenant house to the Schnyder farm. The farm is where Salt Creek takes a large horseshoe bend just east of Waverly. With the horseshoe bend the creek seemed to wrap through the whole farm. That spring it rained so hard that the creek flooded and went out of its banks.

Greener Pastures

The house and the barn were just high enough that the flood waters never came into the house while we lived there. There were times when it came close. I can remember sitting on the back porch and dangling my feet in the shallow flood waters. Salt Creek flooded every spring until 1929 when on a two-year project the Army Corp of Engineers came through with a drag line and straightened the creek from Havelock to Ashland. There were others that weren't so lucky not to have the water get into their place. Dad and I waded down to the bridge where the water was almost up to the bridge planks and from off of the bridge, we pulled chairs and other small pieces of furniture from the flood as it floated by.

The back water from the flood cut us off from town till it went down again. There was a rowboat on the place and Dad would take it over to the George Schnyder place and pick up Ed Andersons. He was the mailman. Dad would row him over to the three-mile corner where his wife's folks lived, and they'd take him around the rest of the route.

The spring of 1922 was also the first year I was old enough to help Dad with the farm work. I had always helped with the chores. I did that since I was big enough to carry a slop bucket to the hogs and scratch out to the chickens. Now I was big enough to drive a team. Before that Dad had let me drive the team back and forth from the barn to the field but I had never worked a team in the field.

Earlier that spring we had gone into Waverly to the sale barn with the intention of buying a good working team. John Munn was sort of the local horse trader and he ran a horse sale in the old sale barn. It was a big wooden shed made out of pine boards with baton strips nailed over the joints. It was little better than the barns most of us knew from home. You made your way in and out through the common barn door that was propped open on sales days with an old piece of fence board. Just inside the doors was a booth where the ladies sold coffee and sandwiches. In the middle, there was a square arena that was formed by the wooden poles that held up the roof. The bleachers were made by stacking straw up around three sides four and five bales high. That gave the people who had come to buy or sell horses somewhere to sit. With all that straw everyone had enough sense not to smoke, but there was a lot of chewing. There were a lot of other people who came to the sale not to buy or sell just cause they were attracted to the sale like flies to manure. The whole place smelled like a combination of old harness, moldy hay, fresh manure, and tobacco split. Maybe that's why Dad my little brother and I went to the sale and left Mom and my sister Olive at home. Whenever you bought a horse at a sale you had to try and use your best judgement. You never really knew what kind of a horse you were getting.

John Munn, who ran the sale, traded horses for a living, just like a used car dealer does cars. Pink Venner and Ira Youngburg were the auctioneers. They ran most every auction that took place in that end of the county in those days. No matter what kind of a sale you went to it was always posted Venner and Youngburg auctioneers.

They always ran the best horses and teams through at the start of the sale while everybody still had lots of money. Later on, they would run the older horses and the wild ones that weren't broke yet. They wouldn't go for as much money. Toward the end of the sale, Dad bought a team of mares that were almost twenty. They didn't bring much, and that's what we started farming with that spring.

On the farm, just across the creek, we had about a fifteen-acre patch that was still native prairie. Nobody had ever plowed it up. That prairie grass was what we used for hay ground. Since everything was done with horses you had to put up plenty of hay to keep them through the winter. I started driving the team pulling a dump rake to wind-row hay.

Three days before Dad had already mowed the hay down so all I had to do was to drive across the field and every time I came to a windrow, I stepped on the trip lever. When you stepped on the trip it started turning the long rod on the rake and meshed with the slant teeth that were on the inside of the hub. When the rod turned with the wheels it raised the teeth on the rake as the wheels turned. As soon as it reached the top of the dump it went back down by itself.

I got along just fine with the old team the first couple of times I raked hay. I even started to get windrows that were halfway straight. Then when we were on the second cutting that year; and I had pert nearly half the hay field raked into wind rows; I was turning the team around at the fence line to take another pass, when a damned Jackrabbit run out of the fence line right at the horses and just scared them all to Hell. They lunged forward and threw me off the back of the rake, just missing the teeth. The team charged into the fence row and one of the mares jumped the fence. In one wild movement, they turned and charged off straddling the fence row. They ran like crazy clipping off fence posts with the rake and tearing up barbed wire until they bound up enough wire in the rake to pull them down. That was a team of horses that you couldn't get to break into a run if you whipped em. If you scare a horse, you can't get em to stop for nothing.

That wasn't the last time I had a round with runaway horses. Dad decided that now that he had a boy old enough to farm he needed another team of horses. The two of us went over to see old John Munn again. As it happened John had a team of harness mules standing in the horse lot that he had just traded for. They looked like a pretty damned good pair of animals. They were a matched set and gave the appearance they could pull harness all day. Everybody always said you could do more work with a mule than you could with a horse. Dad and John started in arguing over the price and after about a half hour of bickering back and forth, we drove a matched team of harness mules back to the Salt Creek Farm.

Every horse has its own temperament and it's the same with mules. Some are spookier than others. Some you can't hardly spook, and others are nervous sons of a guns. These mules were as good of a team of harness mules as you could find, but damn, they spooked easily. It was late summer after the wheat had been thrashed. We were out in the field where there was a big pile of straw still left standing from the thrashing machine. We brought it in as we needed to clean out the pig stalls in the barn. We had the mules hitched to a hay rack standing alongside the straw pile. I was up on the rack stacking straw as Dad pitched it up. We hadn't got more than a fourth of the rack filled when something spooked the mules. They rared up, stamped the ground once for footing, lunged forward into their harness, and took off running. Dad caught the back of the rack and climbed on as it went by. I had fallen down into the hay and couldn't get my footing to get up with the hay rack charging along. Dad drug himself up to the front of the rack and got hold of the reigns. He tried to stop the team but a team of runaway mules you can't stop for nothing.

Greener Pastures

They're either going to run till they wear out or something really big blocks their path. Dad got them turned and they dragged the hay rack in a tight circle till they finally came to a stop. We let them stand there and snort fire for a while, panting heaving, and stamping the ground before we moved back to the straw pile. Most of what we had already forked on the mules had scattered across the field. They were still half-spooked when we finally backed up to the straw pile again. We got back to work pitching straw and by the time we had the rack half full had worked up a decent sweat. We were both busy pitching when some bird or some crazy little thing like that spooked the mules again. I threw my pitchfork, still full of straw off the rack so I didn't land on it as I fell back into the straw. Dad dropped his fork and grabbed for the back of the rack. He missed it this time and fell to the ground. I was lying on my back in the middle of the rack being pulled by a team of charging mules. Dad got up and started running but the mules even pulling a hay rack easily outpaced him. With fire in their eyes, they took off at a dead run across the field running for the road. I got myself pulled up to the front and got hold of the reigns, but it didn't make any difference. The mules had their bits clenched hard in their teeth and no little kid was gonna pull them down. We broke across the field and into the pasture toward the road. The only thing in their way was the wire gate at the end of the pasture before they broke onto the road. The mules busted through the wire gate and turned the corner toward home at a dead run. The only thing hitting the gate did was make them run harder. By now it was all I could do just to stay on the rack let alone try and pull them down. When we stampeded across the wooden bridge it sounded like a cavalry charge as the mule's iron shoes cut into the bridge planks. We charged on and made the turn into the driveway somehow without turning over. The mules still on a dead run were headed for the barn. The barn kept getting closer as the mules charged on. All I could see was the common barn door on the side, just wide enough to lead a horse in and out of and we were running for it, a team of mules and a hay rack. When we hit the barn one of the mules made it in. The other tore the harness and broke loose ending up outside the barn. The tongue on the rack busted to hell, like a matchstick, and the rack and I slammed into the side of the barn. The mules stood there panting and snorting while I got up and started running up the drive toward the road. I saw Dad coming across the bridge as hard as his heavy work boots would let him run. He stopped running out of breath when he saw I was alright.

Amazingly other than the tongue and the harness nothing else was busted. I wasn't hurt and somehow the mules must have hit the wire gate so hard that it just snapped. They didn't even have wire cuts on em. The straw, well it was spread across the field and down the road to the barn. We took the mules back to John and traded for a younger team of horses. Dad sort of gave me the older team and we farmed with horses from then on. It would be a long time before another mule ever set foot on one of our farms.

SPRING OF 1924

When the songbirds came back that spring, we moved off the Salt Creek Farm. This time leaving was our choice. The Salt Creek Farm had been a good way for us to get back on our feet after our hard luck in Oregon. But the lack of farmable land had its disadvantages. Finally, Uncle Lou's farm was without a tenant. The couple who had been living there had found a place of their own to buy and was moving off. Mom and Dad had known for a while that the home place was going to be open. I guess that's why they hadn't been out beating the bushes trying to find a farm of their own.

Great-granddad Tigert had homesteaded there back in the later part of the 1870's. Mom and all of her brothers and sisters had been born there. As far as Mom was concerned the move to Uncle Lou's farm, was just coming home again. It was pretty close to the same for Dad. He'd spent many an evening on the porch when he was courting Liddia, his first wife. I was thirteen when we moved in and we wouldn't leave till I was 21. I grew to be a man walking behind a team, cultivating its fields. My younger brothers and sisters were born there. And it was there I watched them grow up. I never thought of another place I ever lived as home. At least not in the same way as I did Uncle Lou's place.

The old homestead ran along the south side of the DL&D (Detroit, Lincoln, and Denver) highway. The house was a good way south of the highway down the section road. Granddad had planted a grove of cottonwood trees that followed the section road for better than forty rods. They followed the section road clear down to the driveway ending at the turn-in. Just back from the road stood a two-story white frame house. Most of the trees are gone now, knocked down by high wind or lightning. There are only four or five of them left standing now. They're not much more than hollowed-out shells waiting their turn to go down in a strong windstorm. Kind of a sad reminder of what once was.

The summer we moved there I started working from dawn to dusk. I had always worked from the time I was big enough to carry a water bucket, just that now it was all day. I'd already worked plenty of full days in the field at thrashing time. Now it was every day, cept if it was too muddy to get in the field.

Even though we had moved from the Salt Creek Farm we still thrashed with the Walker boys. We had moved a little closer to their place. The summer of 1924 was the first summer I didn't have to be a water monkey. To start with the well water on our place was good drinking water and didn't have to be hauled in. More important was that now my little brother, Charlie, was old enough to drive the pony cart. I moved on to driving a bundle rack when we trashed.

Greener Pastures

The Walker boys owned the machine and seeing as how it was their machine, they decided how things were going to be done. They decided who had to supply what based on how much wheat you had planted that year. Most of the time we had to supply two bundle racks and two drivers. The Walker boys were kept busy enough just running the machinery, so it was up to everybody else to do the rest. We also had to make a cash payment. I think it was about 2 cents an acre. That was to cover the kerosene and repairs on the machine.

The first couple of years before my little brother was old enough to drive a bundle rack were the hardest. Dad and I had to get the corn in and cultivated before the trashing was to start. Once Charlie was old enough to drive a bundle rack if we hadn't gotten the corn scratched over a third time Dad could keep working in the field while Charlie and I took to thrashing.

Some of the farmers who didn't have enough kids to help, or who just plain farmed too much land, had to hire help on to put up their share. There were always a lot of kids who came out from town to work on the thrashing crews. Running a bundle rack got to be damn hard work and hot too. Some of those July afternoons were hotter than Billy Hell. Riding the rack, you had to drive it out to the field where the wheat was shocked up and pitch the rack full with a fork. As soon as you were full you drove it back to the thrasher and pitched it into the machine. It was hard enough for us farm kids who were used to a

Greener Pastures

hard day's work to keep going all day, but for those town kids, it was worse.

Now the Walker boys had a 32-inch thrashing machine. They'd put a board right down the center of the opening so that you could pitch against it from either side. That way two racks could unload at the same time. They kept that machine running all day long, except when they shut it down to check something. The only time you got a break was if the machine got stoked. If you threw too many bundles in headfirst too fast, the thrashing machine would get all plugged up. Then everything had to be shut down and the side panels taken off so the machine could be cleaned out. You could get to about half of it from the side panels but for the rest of it, somebody had to crawl up into the machine and dig the bundles out. On a lot of crews, it would have been a good way to get a break. The Walker boys didn't see it that way. They figured if you were the one that stoked the machine you had to clean it out. I can't remember a day of thrashing when it wasn't hot out and a machine that had been running all day had built up a lot of heat. It was hotter than Billy Hell in there. It didn't take but once and them town kids learned to be damned careful not to stoke the machine, at least not when they were thrashing with the Walker Boys.

That fall, Olive and I started into the sixth grade. I remember that year particularly because that was the last year that Alvi Vega came to school. The Vegas were full-blood Mexicans. They lived in a little shack just west of where you turned off the highway to go to Waverly's south side. The shack was on one of the Walker boy's farms. It didn't have any yard, cause the Walker boys farmed right up next to it. Alvi's Dad worked on a track crew with the railroad. That put him away from home a lot. Alvi was the oldest of six kids and had to run things while his Dad was gone. What made Alvi different than the rest of us kids was that he had started school a couple of years late. That made him the biggest in the class. Being so big and all he had always been kind of the leader. At noon we played baseball, on the ball diamonds north of the school next to the road. We'd choose up sides like you do and if I could I'd always try to be on Alvi's team. He always did the pitching, but nobody ever wanted to catch. So I got my start in catching cause nobody else wanted to. I started to like it and made that my position. I never played much of any other position, and I played ball for some thirty-odd years.

I got along pretty good with Alvi most of the time. There was once that I didn't though. I don't even remember what it was all about anymore, but we got into it. The two of us started to fight and Alvi pulled out a knife and slit my arm open. I laid my old hard work boot right between his legs and dropped him. That ended that. They drove me into the doctor's office in Havelock to get my arm stitched up. Alvi went to the principal's office where he got a pretty good talking to. After that, we never had another problem between us.

We played baseball till it turned cold out. Then we played soccer, snow or no snow. That is the kids that weren't afraid of being outside in the cold. Some of the more sissy kids played marbles down in the gym. Most of the farm kids played outside. We played soccer all winter till it was warm enough to play baseball again.

When the first cold days of late fall came and the ground stayed crunchy hard with frost till almost noon, it was time to put up some meat. Indian summer had come and gone and most of the corn was in the crib. We were done with the fieldwork for the year. All summer long we had worked the fields from dawn to dusk. If you wanted to you could keep working picking corn till the snow fell. There was always someplace where you could hire out to. During the summer there certainly hadn't been any time to put up meat. By now most everybody was out of canned or smoked meat.

When breakfast was over and the chores were out of the way, Dad and I set about to butcher a hog. We always slaughtered a hog first because they were less work than butchering a cow or a steer. That way you could have meat on the table again. I can still remember that hard stomping sound that our work boots made on the porch boards as we left for the feedlot. The screen door seemed to slam extra hard as it closed against the house.

Greener Pastures

My breath rolled away from me like smoke in the cool morning. There was death in the air before we even left the house. Still, the guilt hog had no idea what was waiting for him.

Dad dug a lasso out of the tool shed and hung it across the shoulder of his work jacket. The pigs were used to having us moving around them in the lot, so it wasn't that hard to slip a rope between the hog's legs and tie a knot in it. Once you tied a loop in the rope and pulled it tight the pig would start moving around. I kept the other pigs away from the gate while Dad and the hog slipped through. The hog trotted through looking for adventure. I closed the gate and picked up a big stick to guide him up to the corncrib with while Dad held him back a little with the lasso. You didn't want him to take off running. Up in the corn crib, there was a small pile of corn on the floor to keep him occupied while Dad tied his leg to a post. A lot of people used a gun to kill the pig and a lot of people killed them right there in the lot and stuck to bleed. We never did that cause then you had to fight the other pigs away from the carcass or they'd start in eating on it. Also, then you had to drag it out with a horse. It was easier just to drop em right where you were going to butcher them.

Like I said a lot of people used a gun, but Dad used a big old steel hammer. When the Moment was right Dad swung the blacksmith's, hammer hitting him hard right in the middle of the head. If the pig ever felt anything you'd never have known it, because he dropped dead and never moved. Dad took an iron butcher knife and slit down the juggler. The blood poured out turning the half-frozen dirt into sticky steamy mud. While the blood was still oozing out of his throat Dad stuck the knife through each of his hind legs between the tendon and the bone so he could slip the hooks from a single tree into each leg. Now we just had to snap a block and tackle into the ring on the single tree and hoist him upward toward the rafters so he could finish bleeding out. By now the ground was sloppy with blood. It never bothered anybody though cause you'd seen it all before.

Mom and my sister Olive had come out just after we did to get a fire started under the iron kettle we had set up on blocks in the yard. We filled it with water and let the hog hang till the water was ready to boil. I rolled a wooden barrel under the hog so he could be dropped down into it. We set up a couple of planks on top of two sawhorses to make a crude table to work on next to where the hog was hanging. When the water started to boil Dad took a poker and pushed the coals aside so we could get to the kettle. You had to be damned careful not to get yourself burnt with the scalding water as we carried buckets up to the corncrib to fill the barrel half full of scalding water. By the time the water was ready, he was pretty well bled out.

Dad lowered him down headfirst into the barrel two or three times till the hair was loose. Then he hauled him

Greener Pastures

back up and stuck him in the head with a hay hook so I could drag him onto the table while Dad lowered him down. Dad took the hay hook and ran it through his jaw so we could hoist him back up by the head and dip his hind end into the barrel. When he was all scalded, we hung him back up by his hind legs so we started scrapping the hair off. If you didn't have a skinning bell you could use a dull knife to scrape the hair off. A skinning bell looked like an upside-down saucer with a heavy handle on it. A bell made short work of scraping down a hog.

With the hog's rear hanging about shoulder height Dad took a knife and cut the head off. He laid it over on the table where the dogs couldn't get to it and started to cut the entrails out. He started at the ass and cut down just far enough that the first intestines could be pulled out. The bigger ones were washed out and saved to use for sausage. The little ones went right back out to the rest of the hogs. As you cut further down you had to be careful not to slit the bile sack. If it got on the meat, it would ruin it. The liver, the heart, and everything you wanted to keep you put into a couple of clean buckets as it came out. The worst thing about butchering was you knew that you were going to have to eat liver for the next couple of days.

With the belly clean Dad took an ax and chopped through the breastbone. Now we could let the carcass down a little bit so he could saw down the backbone with a meat saw. If we couldn't borrow a meat saw, we used a carpenter's saw with coarse teeth. The meat saw worked better cause it had a stiff back. Cutting it in two gave you two halves that were easier to handle when you cut it up. Unless you were a big man, half a hog was about all you wanted to carry. All that was left to do was to splash down the meat to clean off the blood and let it hang till morning. We carried the head and entrails to the house where Mom would boil the head to make headcheese and clean the intestines for sausage when we cut the meat up in the morning.

In the morning after chores, we cut up the rest of the hog. Most everything was used. The belly we cut into bacon, which made the breakfasts after butchering the best. The legs we cut off and smoked into hams, and the rest we canned or ground up for sausage. After the hams were smoked, we tied them up from the rafters in the grain bin where the cats couldn't get to them to hang till we were ready for them. That first hog would get you through till you had all the corn picked and time enough to butcher a steer.

Once winter came to the farm there was always a little less work that you had to do. There were always the chores and some repair work that had to be done if it weren't too cold. Once the creek froze over hard and the ice was thick Salt Creek began to take on a social life of its own. In the days before the dragline came through and cut a straight channel, Salt Creek took its lazy time

Greener Pastures

as it wound its way down to the Platte River. It was a wider, slower, friendlier river. Except of course when the spring rains made it swollen and angry. Just west of Waverly the creek used to make a big horseshoe bend. The backwaters that it caused made a narrow lake better than half a mile long. People used to come from all around to go ice skating there. Ice skating was one of the few things that was free. In a time when nobody had any money to spend, much less on recreation or entertainment something free was the only kind you could have.

Just about any afternoon that wanted, if you walked down to the backwaters there would be a group of skaters out on the ice. The shallow banks were covered with trees. They were even thicker around the horseshoe bend. It made it kind of romantic like a lake in the middle of the forest and not just some creek that drained flatland farm ground. With all the thick trees and brush there was always plenty of wood to keep a fire going on the bank to warm frozen fingers, toes, and posteriors. People walked out from town or even drove buggies from nearby farms to get out on the ice. Children raced each other among and around the skaters while their parents skated at a more casual pace. Young couples came and skated off to the more secluded bends of the creek. In those days you didn't have shoe skates, all anybody had were clamp-on skates that you tied onto your shoes or boots. When I was little, I had a pair of double runners so that I wouldn't fall over. Part of growing up was trading in the double runners for a set of single runners.

In the Middle of February when the winter was at its coldest, the ice was at its thickest. It seemed hard to think of the hot days of July that would be coming, but that's what we had to do. Any hard work that was more easily done by a group generally was. Cutting ice was no exception. We cut ice with the same bunch that we thrashed with. Everybody pitched in together to help everyone else make it through the year. That's the way things were then, help your neighbor out and they helped you. Everybody traded work cause there wasn't any money to pay with anyway. There were ice trucks that came out from the icehouses in town but that you had to pay for. So, when the air was the coldest and the ice was the hardest, we cut ice and hauled it into our icehouses.

Most everybody had an icebox and most of them had the same size opening, eighteen by eighteen by thirty inches. Ice was cut by hand. The first thing that had to be done was to scratch out on the ice the line that was going to be sawn. Dad and the other men took turns sawing off the ice. An ice saw worked pretty well but after you had cut a few chunks you were ready to let someone else cut for a while. After to first few blocks had been pulled up out of the water it became a little easier because you didn't have to saw out the whole block. You could cut a line a little longer than the block you wanted and take an ax and chop it loose. It would split right off and float out into open water where the other men would push it to the bank with long pikes. There you could grab it with ice tongs and pull it up onto the ice. The men built a crude wooden chute so the ice could be hauled up the bank and into the wagons. They had a pair of ice tongs that they sunk deep into the block that had a rope tied onto it. Up on the bank, the rope was tied onto a horse, so the horse walked the blocks up the chute. It was high enough that you could back a triple-box wagon right up to it and slide the ice right in. You didn't want to lift any more ice than you had to cause they generally weighed from ninety to a hundred pounds. When the wagons were full, we broke up for the day and everyone drove their wagon full of ice, back to their Icehouses. Some of the families lived three and four miles away, so even the horses got a hard workout hauling a couple of tons of ice over snow-packed roads. There was still plenty of work left to get the blocks into the house. The icehouse wasn't a house at all but rather a roof. The walls didn't come up more than a foot or two above ground. They just needed to be tall enough to support the roof. The rest of the house was dug deep into the ground, like a shallow well. The center beam was probably the most important part of the house because that's where the pulley hung that you used to lower the blocks down into the ground. The ice was slid out of the wagon and lowered down into the icehouse onto a bed of straw.

Then straw was packed around it. In between each layer of ice was another layer of straw. You kept packing straw and ice until it was full.

Eight families sawed ice together. Which meant eight ice houses to fill. All that cutting and hauling is probably what caused George Schnyder to rig up an old Model T motor to a thirty-six-inch buzz saw. He set the motor the saw and a gearbox all up on a couple of skids so the motor could be belted up to the saw. After that, all we had to do was push the saw along and drag the ice out as it broke off. That took all the work out of sawing ice. From then on, we filled all the icehouses in less than a week.

I can still remember what it was like crawling down into the icehouse on Sunday morning before we went to church. It was the middle of July and by ten in the morning, it was already sweltering. Not down in the icehouse. It was a whole different dark cool damp world. There was a lot of straw on top and you had to dig a long way before you could get the tongs into the ice. My little brother Charlie would help me pull it up out of there and lift it into the coaster wagon. We'd wrap it up in a double gunnysack to protect it from the hot July sun while we drug it back to the house. After it got drug up to the house Dad would load it into the ice chest. When we got back from church Dad would churn ice cream in the six-quart freezer. While I was sitting in church, I couldn't think of anything except that big bowl of homemade ice cream I was going to have after Sunday dinner. It was all made from fresh cream and eggs. Mom would get out some strawberries or sometimes we crack open some black walnuts. That's still the best Ice cream I ever had.

Then again there never was much store-bought stuff around. When I went to school Mom always made my lunch. I took lunch in a half-gallon syrup pail. It was always something Mom had made for me she was always baking something. I don't remember how old I was before I tasted baker's bread.

We still heated with firewood, and we would for a good many years. The last thing Dad would do at night before he went to bed was to throw in a knotty piece of wood and cover it up with ashes. That way in the morning there'd be enough coals left to get a fire up. He'd shake the ashes down into the ash pan and put a bucket of cobs on the coals to get the stove heated up. My job was to go get water from the well to fill the reservoir although no one had ever told me to do it, I just did it. I was always the first one to make footprints in the fresh snow. By the time Mom came down to get breakfast started the kitchen would be warm and there'd be hot water in the reservoir.

Once a week we ground wheat to have fresh creme of wheat. There were always fresh eggs and bacon from the smokehouse. Fruit and potatoes from the cellar. That was one thing we always had was a good breakfast.

There was just enough time left to get the chores done before the Model T school bus came to cart us off to school.

We never had much trouble getting out in the winter. We lived on the mail route, so the road was plowed. Bill Cook pulled a drag for the county by the house. It was made out of bridge planks stacked two high in the shape of a vee. He hooked up five horses abreast, like you do for farming, and cleared a single lane. He and Dad knew each other from way back. When he got to our drive, he'd turn down our lane and turn a circle around at the barn, so we could always get out. He was a pretty good fellow and even though I thought he did it special for us I suppose he did it for just about everybody.

The one thing there was seldom enough of was firewood. When we lived on the Salt Creek farm we never hurt for firewood. Here on Uncle Lou's farm, there wasn't anything for trees cept the cottonwood windbreak. Cottonwood wasn't bad for burning if you cut in while the tree was alive. If you waited till it died it wasn't nothing more than a shell left for burning. We couldn't exactly be cutting down Granddad's windbreak, so like everybody else around, we burnt a heck of a lot of corncobs. They burned hot and fast. They weren't worth much for keeping a fire going but they were free, `and they were easy to get.

Greener Pastures

Somehow, we got by with cottonwood and corncobs until 1928. That was the year that the Army Corp. of Engineers came through with a dragline and straightened out the old Salt Creek channel. They cut a new Channel clear from Havelock to Ashland. I had been dating a girl off and, on that year, whose older brother and another kid had gotten the job of cutting the trees down off the banks ahead of the dragline. They had to cut the banks clear and pull the trees and brush back from in front of the machinery. A neighbor kid, whose family was in the same boat as we were for not having firewood, and I, made a deal with my girlfriend's brother. We'd saw up the firewood for them and give them back a share of what we cut.

By 1928 we had acquired a tractor. Dad let me drive it over to where we were cutting wood. We got hold of a buzz saw that we hooked up to the belt pulley on the tractor. The old cottonwood and creek willows we'd just pile up and burn. The rest of the good trees we'd saw up and to make cordwood out of them. Every morning we hooked a couple of wagons onto the back of the tractor to drive over to where we were cutting. It was a strange thing. During a time of honesty, when you never thought twice about leaving your car or your house unlocked, you took everything that you had cut home with you. It didn't matter if you stacked it up or just left it lying around. In the case of firewood, since everybody burnt it if we didn't take it all home with us when we left at night there was a damn good chance it wouldn't be there in the morning. It was a lot of hard work but then everything was. We cut and sold a lot of firewood that year. I took a lot home too. My share of wood that I took home kept us in firewood for three years. That was a lot of cut wood.

In high school, we did a lot of sawing too, just not for firewood. We had a pretty good shop class. We started out making nail boxes and the like. I've still got mine. I've got Charlie's too. Most of the farm kids already knew how to use a saw, a square, or a hammer, and the town kids, well they learned to do a better job. Even though Waverly was a pretty good-sized town, there were still more farm kids than there were town kids in school. The last couple of years in high school, we made wagon boxes. There were very few machinery sheds back then. Most everybody had to let their machinery sit outside. Wagons don't last forever when they sit out in the weather. There was always a good demand for a well-made wagon box or a hayrack. We only made the boxes. Usually, the running gear on a wagon was still in good shape. The box set over it and protected it from the weather.

We also had a hell of a good FFA Class. George Speidel was the instructor. He was known all over the state for what he knew about farming. The university tried and tried to get him to come and teach at the Ag College, but George wanted to stay in a small school. He also kind of

Greener Pastures

thought he wanted to stay in Waverly. We learned how to feed livestock, and we studied out of university books on nutrition. We learned how to make cattle gain weight and how to take care of horses. Taking care of horses was pretty important back in the late twenties. There weren't many tractors around but more important was the fact that tractors burnt kerosene. That cost money. It was only 5 cents a gallon but that was cash. Horses and mules ate hay and grain. Two things that didn't cost you anything out of your pocket. What did cost was buying the team. A team of horses could run from $100 to $300 depending on how good a team they were. Some people preferred to use mules. Mules could take the heat a lot better. For the most part, you didn't have to risk overworking a mule like you did a horse cause a mule would just stop. He'd stop and he wouldn't move until he was ready to go again. A horse on the other hand you had to rest so that you wouldn't break them down. If there's one thing that tractors changed about farming, it's how often you took a break. Not so much to rest yourself, but to rest the team. At least not for a couple of young bucks like my brother Charlie and I we didn't need as many breaks as the horses did. There wasn't a whole lot you could do while the team rested so we played catch. We always took our gloves and a ball to the fields. Charlie liked to pitch. Myself, ever since the days of Alvi Vega I'd been a catcher. So, Charlie would pitch a way to me till we decided that the team couldn't rest anymore, and we'd take to farming again. I don't know what we'd have done without baseball back then to get through the long summers. Everything we did was baseball. The only reason we didn't balk when Dad sent us into the field was cause we knew we were going to throw some ball. Even picking corn had some element of baseball involved because we practiced pitching while throwing ears of corn into the wagon. It wasn't just picking corn; it was baseball practice.

Baseball was pretty close to home too. The Waverly town team used to play ball in Uncle Lou's pasture. We didn't have far to walk to see the games. There were some pretty good players too. I can remember when old Carl Swanson played ball in our pasture. Town teams, that was amateur baseball at its finest. The Waverly town team fell apart though when I started high school. They just couldn't keep enough players to field a team. I guess after six days of working in the fields and even on Sundays you had chores, some guys were just too tired to go play ball on Sunday afternoon. Everybody milked a few cows back then. You'd have to get done playing ball and go home to do the milking.

The only ball around for a few years was the school team. The only good thing about the town team falling apart was that they gave the uniforms and the bats and balls to the school. Baseball also got us out of some school. On Friday afternoon the guys that played on the ball team were excused to go play. I had a driver's license, cost 75 cents, and was good for life, or at least it was

Greener Pastures

supposed to be. The state treasury got 25 cents out of each license. On Friday Dad would let me drive the old Model T to school. All the other days I had to ride the bus. The boys from Rock Creek would drive into town on game days. Same thing with the Bray boys from out of Prairie Home. They had a brand-new Model A they brought into town on game days. Rock Creek and Prairie Home just went to grade school in their schools. For high school, they came to Waverly. Once everybody was suited up, we headed off down the gravel roads to meet our advisory. We would get there after half-hour to an hour of eating dust from a dirt road. Win or lose we drove straight back to school to shower up and change. Most of us were farm kids and had to hightail it back home to get chores done. Didn't anybody have any time to go out helling around. After you got done with the chores you went to bed.

I didn't always have to ride the bus though. Once we were in high school a few of the boys got to drive the car to school and back. I guess their Dads figured that would get them home to help on the cores sooner. We went to bed early in the fall and winter. The sun went down around six O'clock. Most of us were just finishing up chores at dusk. Electricity wouldn't come to rural Nebraska for a good many years yet, so we had to eat supper by the light of a lantern. I started running around with the neighbor boy, who lived a little north of us on the other side of the highway. They had a 1924 Dodge with a two-speed transmission. He'd give me a ride if we had to stay around school for something and the bus had already gone. We never had to worry about the highway, cause that was gravel. Our road was another story. If it was frozen, we didn't have to worry. We could bounce down the ruts and get home. If it wasn't then we'd have to hope, we could churn our way through. When it rained the ruts grew deeper than the grader ditch. The ditches couldn't have been too deep though cause I used to turn the team around on the road when I pulled the go-dig through the corn. The ruts though, were so deep you didn't have to steer. The car could guide itself down the road. If we got stuck, we'd both get out and push. If we couldn't get the car out, we'd leave it sit till morning. Then if it hadn't rained again, we'd get the team out before we started chores and pull it out. We never had to worry about flooding, like we did on the Salt Creek place, but seemed like except for July, we always had plenty of mud.

It was a good thing too because the whole town seemed like, come to our place for Fourth of July. It all started back a spell when the town team used to play baseball in Uncle Lou's pasture. The whole world lived for baseball back then. It only made sense that there would be a game of some sort on the fourth of July. Everybody came. Pretty soon it turned into the town pick-nick and for as long as we were around the fourth of July was in our pasture. People could park their cars in the shade of the old cottonwood trees and spend the day watching baseball, playing games, and having pick-nicks. Weren't nobody ever said that we were going to have the town party at our place it just sort of happened that way.

The other bit of excitement was the state fair. If we could get five dollars saved up by fair time, Dad would let us take the car to the fair. Charlie and I and a couple of the neighbor boys would spend the week at the fair. We took along a Sears and Roebuck tent and set it up to camp in. A lot of people did that. There was a pretty good-sized tent city set up on the fairground. It cost twenty-five cents to get in. Once you were in, you didn't have to pay again. You could get a pass to go out and come back in. As long as you made it back in before midnight your pass was still good, and you didn't have to pay again. In the evening we'd go out and do a little Helling around town, but we were always careful to be back before midnight, so we didn't have to pay.

We used to leave everything that we had brought with us in the tent. Never once did we have to worry about anybody going into the tent and taking anything. People didn't do things like that then. You stayed out of what wasn't yours. We used to leave our money lying in the tent and never gave it a second thought. But when the fair ended so did our vacation from chores and we'd have to pack it up and head back home again.

Greener Pastures

As I said before Uncle Lou's farm was about the only place, I had that I could call home. I was thirteen years old when we moved there, and I was twenty-one when we left. We left by choice, not because we had to. That is in a way anyhow. You see it was 1932. It wasn't a good year for farming, but we were ok. What happened was that things hadn't gone well for my Uncle Lou. Not well at all. He had borrowed some money at the Lancaster bank in Waverly against the farm. This year he just didn't have anything to make a payment with. It wasn't wrong that they took it over. The bank just had the right to take the farm on default. The bank foreclosed and had a sale. We could have bought it at the sale, but it went for far too much for us. It was bought by a man we called Hog Anderson. I don't remember his real name cause everybody called him Hog. They called him that cause he always wanted everything for himself. He'd been that way even back in high school they said. He and his brother were president and vice president at the bank. They were just a couple of damned greedy old Swedes. He and his brother already owned half the county north of Waverly. They were straight Swedes. I suppose there wasn't anything underhanded about it. It sure seemed that way. He being president of the bank and all, forced the sale and then bought it for himself. Old Hog even said that we could stay on the place as renters for as long we wanted, cause he was going to be renting the place out and we would be good renters. Dad said we would have gone ahead and stayed there if anybody else would

64

Greener Pastures

have bought the farm. Old Hog had a habit of trying to tell everybody what to do. What they ought to be raising and how they ought to be going about it. Dad said he just wasn't going to stay around and let old Hog boss over us that way.

We did what all too many farmers in the county did that year. We got a hold of Verner's auction and had a sale. We kept a lot of our things. We sold some of the extra farm equipment and some of the household things. It wasn't a huge sale. A lot of the things we would be taking with us.

That fall it didn't take that long for us to pick out our corn. I was out of school so what little corn we had was put away in a short time. We didn't have much for chores to do. All we had kept was one old milker to keep us till we left. There was nothing to keep us in Nebraska for the winter, we packed up and left for Iowa.

IOWA DAYS

We moved onto a farm just outside of Allerton Iowa. There wasn't much to do, moving on to a farm in late fall. Charlie and I hired out picking corn to earn enough cash to make it through the winter. When the farm work played out, we got ourselves onto the town basketball team. We traveled around to all the other little towns around playing against their town teams. It gave us something to do that we liked. It was good because we got to know a lot of the folks around that way. We played basketball every winter for the town after that. There were two different winters when the Harlem globetrotters came through. They were out barnstorming the countryside, trying to make some money. They'd stop in the little towns and play an exhibition game against the town team. Everybody would come from all around to watch. We had a packed gym. The town team didn't stand a chance in hell against them fellows. Just one of them could dribble the whole team silly. No matter how hard we tried, they just made us look like a bunch of clowns.

With the team's share of the money, we went to see the State basketball championships at the end of the winter. Dad let me take the Model A to drive a bunch of us the 100 miles over to Des Moines Iowa to watch the games. It cost us 25 cents to get into the gym. We had enough left to buy a meal and pay for the gas to get home.

Greener Pastures

Allerton Iowa was the timothy grass capital of the world. All of the farms around had a patch that they let go to seed for cash money. We were damn lucky that we had kept the power binder. Binding Timothy grass was what kept us going. It was the first cash money we would get in the farming season. Timothy grass was a lot harder to bind than wheat or oats. You had to move damned slow, so you didn't lose half of it. All of the farmers over there still had horse drawn binders. A horse-drawn binder was driven by a jack-wheel on the underside of it. The horses had to run the whole thing. The biggest horse-drawn binder they made was 7 feet long. It was big enough that you had to have five strong horses to pull it. Most farmers didn't have that many working horses. Almost everybody who had horse-drawn machines pulled a five-foot binder.

Our binder ran off the power take-off on the tractor. Dad had bought a new ten-foot power binder in the late twenties when they first came out. It was the best thing we could have done not letting it go on the sale. Timothy was ready to bind right after the oats were cut and bound. With the ten-foot binder, we had the oats cut and our timothy grass bound while the neighbors were still cutting oats. We had a couple of neighbors and each one of them had eighty acres of timothy grass. As luck would have it, they were running behind and asked us if we would help them get it in. Dad told Charlie and me we could have the money as long as we paid for the gas and oil and any repairs that were needed. That way we could earn a little extra money. The neighbors furnished the twine, and lunch, and kept cool water coming to us. Charlie and I cut and bound all their timothy grass for $1.25 an acre. We made over a hundred dollars that year with the binder. That was a good deal of money for a couple of young bucks who had never had any money to speak of.

We had been going to a Presbyterian Church that was just outside of Allerton ever since we first moved to Iowa. The Presbyterians had a college down at Tarkio, Missouri. Charlie had decided to use his share of the money to go down there and study math. Charlie was able to pay for his tuition and most of his room and board from cutting Timothy grass with me. It was a good thing; cause Dad wouldn't have been able to help him out any. While I put my share on the bill down at the oil station to pay for what we had used and so we'd have tractor fuel to farm with the rest of the year. We had an old Farmall that burnt kerosene. A lot of people around had John Deeres and they burnt tractor fuel. Tractor fuel was a penny a gallon cheaper than kerosene. But John Deere didn't make anything but the old "D". They didn't make a row crop till 1936. So, we paid a penny more and burnt kerosene in a Farmall row crop tractor.

The corn in the thirties didn't grow any different in Iowa than it did in Nebraska. There just wasn't much rain to be had in either place. Corn grew about three feet tall if you were lucky. If you were even luckier it had ears on it. It would rain enough in the spring just enough to get it started, then it wouldn't rain again. The corn burnt up in the sun during July and August. When it came time to harvest it didn't take any time at all and we had it all picked out. The rest of it we cut and tied in shocks for the cattle, to try to get something out of it. Charlie had already left for college by the time corn-picking time was at hand. I stayed around looking for corn I could hire out to pick. It was the same all around. There wasn't anybody that had enough ears to make it worth hiring somebody to pick it.

Finally, I came across a kid, about my age, by the name of Jess Alley. He had a 1928 model "A" roadster. Just so happened he was trying to find somebody to head up north to help him pick corn. He'd been going up there every fall for several years with another kid to pick corn for this German fellow. This year the other kid up and got himself married. He didn't think he'd better be running off to the other end of the state leaving a new bride behind and all. Jess asked me if I couldn't go along. Said the money would be good and this old boy always had plenty of corn to pick. Jess was about 5'-10" tall, just a little bit shorter than myself. He always wore bib overalls that were about a size too big, like he was waiting to grow into them. Said he liked them that way. He got used to wearing clothes that were too big growing up cause all he'd ever had was hand-me-downs from older brothers or the neighbors. Didn't seem right any other way.

When he showed up to pick me up though, he had on a brown suit, new hat, and freshly polished shoes. I up and asked him if he couldn't wait for a spell while I got my traveling clothes on. I said I hadn't expected him for another hour yet and hadn't gotten dressed. I lied. Dad took him inside and got him a cup of coffee. Mom always had coffee on the stove in the mornings if we were still around the barnyard. Once we were on the road, Jess said he liked to travel in style cause it made you feel important. I think he knew I was planning on going the way I was dressed cause I had my suitcases lined up and ready on the porch. He never said a word though about it. Later on, riding in style would save us from going to jail or at least a good fine. It was a two-hundred-mile drive to get there. I tell you after two hundred miles in a two-seat roadster I was glad to finally pull into the yard of that big white farmhouse. It was surrounded by a grove of elm trees with a few cedars mixed in to stop the winter wind. We were met at the door by a good-sized German Immigrant with a big mustache that hid his top lip. He reached out his hand and bellowed out "Vell Mama look who finally made it. And who's dis fine joung man you got mit ya dis yar?" His wife came a bustling as fast as her big round body would allow, wiping her hands on her apron as she came. I don't think I ever saw her, but she didn't have an apron on. For all I know she slept with one on.

"I been holding dinner for you two and we just about be starved by now." That was the first time I became acquainted with pheasant. She had two big old birds roasted up just waiting for us to eat. We went to work picking corn the next morning. The old boy had sixty-to-seventy-bushel corn. It took us over a month to pick him out. We'd go out in the morning and when we came back in for lunch, we'd have a wagon full of ears. He had an inside elevator to kick the corn up into the crib, so we didn't have to shovel it. Once we were empty, we cleaned up for lunch. The old gal always had a good lunch for us. We never had to worry about that. After lunch, we'd take the team and the wagon back out into the field and pick the wagon full again.

He had three eighty-acre farms and most of it was put to corn. They had three kids, but only one boy. He was already married off and had a farm of his own. Both the two girls still lived at home with them. The oldest taught grade school at the rural school just down the road apiece and the youngest one went into town to go to high school. That left the old boy hiring out to do a lot of things that he needed help with. In the summer there were always plenty of neighbor kids to help out, but once school took over, he needed help picking out the corn. On our way back in from picking corn in the evening, for the last quarter mile we walked down alongside an old hedgerow. It ran all the way down the field and stopped just short of the barnyard. Since it was well into November the sun was coming down into the trees pretty early. As we walked along there were pheasants going up into those trees starting to roost for the night. Why they were just thick in there. There must have been what was close to a couple of hundred of them. Why they were thicker than chickens in a henhouse. It was still before pheasant season had opened up, but Jess had brought along a couple of old single-barrel shotguns. They weren't worth too much, but they worked fine enough. Back then if you got caught the first thing, they used to do was to take away your gun. He brought old guns cause that way if they took the guns they wouldn't be getting much. We never took guns out to pick, cause you never could tell what a horse was gonna do when they heard a gunshot. Late afternoon on Sunday was different. Jess, the old German, and I'd walk out into the hedgerow with our guns just before sunset. Since the season wasn't open yet there wasn't much need to worry about our limit. Getting caught with one was just as bad as getting caught with twenty. We shot up enough pheasant that the old boy got away pretty cheap feeding us. We had pheasant every night of the week.

Fair enough though. We got our room and board and our washing done for free. On top of that, we got three cents a bushel for picking corn. The year before I'd been picking corn for two cents a bushel and had to scoop it into the crib. So, I was feeling pretty good about three cents and not having to scoop it into the elevator. We stayed at home through the week except for Saturdays when we'd go into town. We'd stay out pretty late but still getting home early enough that nothing was ever said about it. I suppose the old boy was half in favor of it cause he always made sure that on Saturday we had some spending money for the weekend. Then when we were all done, and he was picked out he'd settle up with us. Always in cash. We'd head for home with better than a hundred bucks a piece in our pockets feeling like we were on Wall Street.

We always finished picking out his corn in the middle of the week. It happened that way for the three years that I went along. We stayed there until Sunday to travel back. The old boy had five acres of what he called dry corn that he cut for fodder. We'd stay around and help him get it bought in. Dry corn didn't grow quite as tall, maybe only shoulder height. He had a corn binder that cut a swath three rows wide and tied it up into some pretty good-sized bundles. He had it all tied into shocks and standing in the field. All we had to do was throw the bundle up onto the wagons and haul it into the shredder. He'd shear it up, ears and all, and throw it into the haymow for cattle feed. It took quite a few men to run the whole thing cause there had to be a couple up in the barn to scoop it to the sides from where the blower threw it. Two more had to feed it into the shredder and a couple more to run the wagons hauling it all in. Most of the time Jess and I either ran the wagons or forked into the shredder. You moved around a bit, so you didn't have to do the same thing all day long. I never did find out how it happened whether somebody hid it up in there as a joke or if it had crawled up in one of those bundles and died or what the hell happened. His boy and I were throwing bundles into the shredder and a couple of the neighbors were up in the haymow. I threw a bundle into the shredder and could smell it immediately. A damned skunk had gone through the shredder. Those two old neighbor boys come jumping out of the loft never even looking for the ladder. That shredded-up skunk ruined one hell of a lot of fodder. After we could stand to get up in there, we forked out the worst of it and threw it to the hogs. Smell like that is hard to get rid of. I guess it stunk up there all winter long. I was just damned glad I wasn't in the hay mow when that skunk hit the fan.

Sunday morning when we got ready to go, we dressed up a whole crock full of pheasants. Jess and I put them down in the rumble seat to keep them cool on the way home. We headed down the highway all duded up just like we were going to church. A little before sunset we came over this hill where a couple of game wardens had a bunch of cars stopped checking for pheasants. When they stopped us, they looked in the car at us with our suits on and guess they figured we wouldn't have been out hunting dressed like that. They waved us right on through. Who knows what would have happened if they had found that crock full of dressed birds. When we stopped a little way down the road to buy gas, I bought a Sunday paper. On the front page, there was a picture of a grader ditch along the highway just a ways to the south. It was a picture looking at a ditch full of pheasants at the top of a long hill. Turned out the highway patrol had stopped a car with a headlight out at the bottom of the hill. There were a few problems, and they were sitting there with their lights on for quite a spell. Every car that came along thought that they were checking for game and threw their birds out. I mean to tell you there was a pile of birds in that ditch that looked like a truckload had been spilled out or something.

I may have been rich for the ride home, but when I got there, I gave what I had made to Dad. The family was in need of cash more than I was. The rest of the winter I did what I could to keep us in a little bit of money. There was a neighbor boy who got me to go along with him down to the Missouri border. There was a bunch of sawmills down there. Seemed like every other farm had some kind of a mill set up. If they did any sawing at all they'd have a pile of scabs that they let you have for a little bit of nothing if you hauled them off. His Dad had an old model "T" truck that he let us drive down there. We'd go get a load of scabs and haul them back to his place where there was a buzz saw set up. We pulled them out of the truck and sawed them up for firewood. When the truck was empty, we loaded it all back onto the truck and drove into town to sell it for firewood. We were able to each make five dollars a week after we paid for gas and whatnot if we worked at it.

Come spring we went back to farming. There wasn't anybody wanting to spend cash money on firewood when it was warm enough anyhow. The first thing that was ready to cut was the buckwheat. We had three acres of buckwheat. It wasn't very much, but you didn't want much. Buckwheat grew so short that you couldn't cut it with a binder. You'd end up losing it all. We borrowed a cycle bar mower from the neighbors to cut it with. Dad fastened an old signboard on the bottom of it just below the bar to catch the wheat. When the signboard got full, we'd sweep it off to the side and tie it up by hand. It was a lot of work, but it was worth it. We didn't grow the buckwheat to sell. It was too much work for what little you got off of it. We grew it mainly for our own use. The neighbors all around us had patches of the stuff and had gotten us started with a little seed. What we did do with it was to grind it up for breakfast cereal. We had a 12-inch burr mill that we run it through to grind it up. It did a pretty good job, but it left some coarse stuff that didn't grind up. We took our coarse ground wheat over to the neighbor's place. They had built up a fan mill to shake out the coarse stuff that didn't grind up.

Greener Pastures

Most every morning we had buckwheat pancakes and molasses. Coarse we had chickens, so we had fresh eggs. Everybody kept at least one milk cow for fresh milk. If Mom didn't make pancakes she cooked the buckwheat into fresh cream-of-wheat. Fresh buckwheat tastes a whole lot better than what you can buy in the store. Everything that we ate, we either grew or made. We had a big garden and we always had canned pork. It was a good thing cause the cash crops in the thirties never amounted to anything. We would have starved if we had to have bought our food.

We scratched over the corn with the cultivator, but it never did any good. It never put on enough ears to hardly make it worth picking. The only thing that seemed to hold its own in the dry weather was sorghum. It wasn't a cash crop though. We used it for cattle feed. We had a patch of about four acres of sorghum. We had grown it in Nebraska, so it wasn't anything new, but we hadn't ever done anything with it besides feeding it to the cows. My wood-cutting buddy said his Dad would let us borrow his truck if we wanted to haul some down and have it pressed into Molasses. The corn sorghum was ready to cut in the fall, just before it was time to start picking and shucking corn. If you were going to press it into molasses you had to cut it and get it pressed before there was a frost or a freeze. That affected the taste of it. Most of the sorghum we cut with a corn knife and tied into shocks that we could let stand in the field till we had time to bring it into the barn. Then we could run it through the shredder and tossed it up into the barn. For some of it though we borrowed the truck and loaded it down with shocks to haul to the press. Everyone around us kept a molasses barrel. With no cash to buy things, they used a lot of molasses. You could use it for most of the things you needed sugar for. It made the cookies a bit darker in color, but they tasted good. Charlie and I hauled a couple of truckloads of cane down to the other side of the Missouri border. That was where all the sawmills were that we had been hauling scabs from. They were all just little family-run outfits. Most of them were farmers and sawed wood in the fall and winter. They couldn't sell grain for nothing so I guess maybe they could make a little money selling lumber. When it came time to press sorghum, damned near all the mills would quit sawing and go to pressing sorghum.

If you had a sawmill, you had to have some kind of an engine that you could belt up to the sawmill. Since they already had the engine all they needed was a press to turn. Not everybody had a power press though. We took our cane down to the same old boy where we had been getting the scabs that we cut and sold for firewood. The fellow that ran the mill still had a horse press. A lot of the smaller mills still used horses to press sorghum. It took quite a while to press the juice out. You had to hand-feed it into the press, and it wouldn't take but four stocks at a time. Then you caught it on the other side and loaded it back on the truck to use for cattle feed. We hauled two loads down and took one back. When we got it home, we threw it over the fence for the cows and pigs to finish cleaning up. Once we did our work getting it pressed out then it was the old boy at the mill's turn to do his work. He had a big oval vat with a flat bottom. It kind of looked like a bathtub. It set on the ground, but he had dug a hole underneath it to build a fire in. That way you could still walk around three sides to stir it. You had to keep it stirred and the fire had to be just right. If it weren't it would get scorched. If that happened, then the whole mess tasted burnt and wasn't any good. You had to bring it to a boil real slow and careful like. Once it started to boil it got a scrum of the top of it that constantly had to be scooped off. That was the impurities boiling out of it.

Dad went back down a few days later to pick up our share in a wooden barrel. We didn't have to pay the old boy he just kept back his share for payment. It had to be kept in a wooden barrel, cause a metal one would ruin the taste of it. All you had to do was take the top ring off the barrel to get the top out. Then you could pour it full and put the top back in. The wooden barrels had a two-inch bunghole that you could drive a tap into once you got it to where you wanted it. We kept ours in the wash house. Hot or cold it always poured. Sometimes in the winter you just had to stand there a little longer while you waited for it to come out. We never kept more than

Greener Pastures

a gallon in the house cause it attracted flies. You had to be sure it was closed up tight.

That first year the old buck we took it to did a hell of a good job. We ate up every drop. He was an older fellow, but he wasn't that old. Just the same later that year he up and died. The next fall we had to look for somewhere else to take our cane to get pressed. We found another fellow who would press it out for a share just like we had been doing. Well, he burnt the stuff. We hardly touched it except when we had to. If they burnt it, you could ask for your money back. Since we did it for a share, we were just out that much sorghum. The last two years we were in Iowa we found a couple of brothers that run a mill down on the Missouri side. They did a pretty good job. Didn't burn it or nothing. It still wasn't quite as good as that first barrel that the old man had done for us. That old buck knew how to boil down molasses.

When school let out Charlie would come home to help with the farming. That first year we were in Iowa we tried to get a town team together so we could play baseball. It ran for a while but towards the end of summer, it kind of fizzled out. Everybody was too busy farming to play baseball. I gave up baseball till we moved back to Nebraska again. It was too much work for everybody trying to farm when it didn't rain to have time for baseball, I guess. As it turned out it wouldn't be that long of a wait till I would get the chance to play again. We tried to hang on there in Iowa. But come 1936 we

still hadn't had a decent year yet. Dad lost the farm to
the bank.

Return to Nebraska

It was the week after New Year's Day 1936; Dad and I packed up a couple of suitcases with traveling clothes and gassed up the old car. We were headed for Nebraska. Dad figured that if we could find a farm to rent in Nebraska we could start over again. We still had family and people who knew us there. We never had hard times there, it was just that, if only old Hog hadn't ended up with Uncle Lou's place we'd probably still be there and making it just fine.

There wasn't any hotel or any place to stay in Waverly, so we got a room at the hotel in Havelock. We kind of poked around Havelock for a day or so and back and forth to Waverly. Havelock didn't have a whole hell of a lot going on then. The only thing that was keeping it going was the Burlington Railroad Shops in those days. Out in Waverly though we had a bit of luck. Hike Gilman, who had just bought the lumberyard there was going to be moving into town. He had a decent farm, but he was trying to do the chores on the place and then come into town and run the lumberyard. He was burning the candle at both ends. He hadn't planned on moving into town until March. What probably cinched the deal for us though was that he needed someone to run the place till then. I was willing to stay there and do the farm work for him till he had a chance to have a sale in the spring. Then he'd move to town, and we could take it over. We went out to look the place over with him and get the deal all squared away. Once he and Dad had come to terms on everything Dad left me there and went back to Iowa to take care of the family and what little farm work we still had over there. It would be a couple of months until I would see them again.

The Gilman place was out east of Lincoln at what is now 120th and Havelock Avenue on the south side of the road. All the buildings are gone now, but there was a frame house, a small barn, and a few outbuildings. There was electricity that ran on poles right down the south side of the road, but old Gilman had never wanted to pay to have it wired so there wasn't any electricity. I guess it didn't matter that much though, we'd never had it before. We weren't going to miss what we had never had.

Hike Gilman and his wife had sixteen cows that they'd been milking by hand. I got settled in with them that night, which was pretty early even for me. The next morning, we were up at four getting started for the milking. With it being winter, Hike's wife was all too glad to stay inside and make breakfast. She didn't mind not milking even if it was the last year, they were gonna be doing it. Outside in the barn, it was freezing cold, but the cows had to be milked no never mind. It was still pitch black out and would be for the whole time we milked. We did a lot of things by the light of a lantern. By the time we got the lanterns out and enough hay forked over into the head stalls the cows would be lining up to be let in. Hike and I started out milking together. We would each get four cows milked before he would have to go in and get ready to take off for town. When I finish up milking the other eight cows, I'd kick em all over a bit more hay, close up the milk cans, and take the buckets back to the house to wash them out.

Once I got the buckets washed out and put away, I got myself cleaned up and ready for breakfast. I had plenty of time to eat and what have ya before old Pete Kriner would roll into the barnyard to pick up the milk cans. He had an old flatbed truck with stake sides to keep the milk cans from rolling off. He had himself a pretty good-sized milk route that he drove. He picked up milk from almost all the farmers around and hauled it into Strauss Brothers' Dairy. Since he saw everybody daily, he knew pretty much what was going on and some of the things he shouldn't. He wasn't really a gossip; he just did a good job of making conversation. In some ways it was good cause if you had something that you wanted everyone to know about all you had to do was to tell Pete to spread the word. At the same time, you didn't want to be airing any dirty laundry in front of him cause it might get spread around a bit too.

After breakfast I'd get my old work jacket back on and go out to scoop some silage into the troughs for the dairy cattle. He had a few head of beef yet and I had to tote them some hay and cracked corn. The corn was to help

Greener Pastures

them keep their weight up in the cold weather. I hauled the garbage out to the pigs. They'd eat damn near anything, and that's what we gave em. You always made your best money on the pigs, cause hell they never cost you nothing.

The worst thing about the cold spells was taking care of the water. Whenever it was cold out, even if there was snow on the ground you still had to keep water to the livestock. Everything had to be pumped from the well. At least the damned well over at the Gilman's was close to the barn. That was a little help. If the tank wasn't frozen solid, I'd take an ax and cut the ice off the top so the cows could get to the water. It would stay open long enough that they could get a good drink before it froze back over. I could dip buckets into it and carry water to the hog trough. In February the tank would freeze solid, which made everything harder. First, I had to chop a big enough hole out of the ice to hold water for the cows and fill it with water from the well. If there was enough wind you could take the brake off the windmill and let the pump fill the hole. If there weren't then I'd have to take the bolts out and mount up a handle so it could be pumped by hand. Once I got a handle mounted up, I just left it that way till it warmed up enough to thaw the tank.

I usually had time to come back in and warm up a bit before it was time to go back out and start the four O'clock milking. I'd throw some more hay into the headstalls and if the cows hadn't wandered back in yet

I'd have to go out and call them back in. If I was lucky, I could get done before dark. Most of the time I didn't. I started the day with the light of a lantern and finished it with one.

Old man Kriner only came by to pick up the milk but once a day. If it was cold out, I'd keep the milk in the barn and pile hay all around the cans to keep it from freezing till Pete got there in the morning. He was a creature of habit, not a whole lot of new come out of him. I wonder how many times I heard him say, "Alright where'd ya hide the milk today?"

I stayed there and kept milking till the weather broke. On the first of March, I went back over to Iowa to help with the sale. It wasn't going to be such a big sale. We were going to keep most of the machinery. What we were getting rid of was all the little stuff that wasn't worth the trouble to move. What went on the sale were wooden fence posts, old rolls of wire, boxes of junk, and a few household goods. It wasn't but a half-day sale.

Dad knew a man by the name of Ed Johnson, known him since they were kids. He lived a half a block west of the Modern Woodman Building in Waverly. Ed had a flatbed semi-trailer that he did hauling with. Dad and I brought a load of stuff over from Iowa on a flatbed trailer that was made out of an old Model "T" chassis. That's how almost everything that came back from Iowa was on that old flatbed trailer. There was no way we could haul the machinery back though; we knew that after the first trip. So, we went over to see Ed Johnson and find out what he'd charge us to haul the machinery back from Iowa. He charged us $35 to go a little better than two hundred miles over and back. It was a lot of money back then, but it got all of the machinery back in one trip. I had the money to pay for it cause I'd been getting a dollar a day milking and doing chores for the Gilman's for a couple of months. We were all moved into the Gilman place, and they were moved to town by the end of March.

Charlie was through with college and off on his own now, but my little brother Pud was big enough to help with the crops. I stayed there at home and helped them get the crops in before I decided to hire out and earn a little cash money. The Gilman farm was 120 acres of farm ground so there was plenty of work just getting it put to seed. There wasn't any Timothy grass around though like there had been over in Iowa to run the binder on but there was plenty of wheat that could be bound. Most of the farmers were still trying to scratch over their corn for a third time when the wheat was ready, so it wasn't that hard to talk them into letting me do their binding.

It was just a day or two after the fourth of July, I had gotten the job of binding wheat on the Jacoby farm just down the road. That day I had just finished up with one neighbor in the morning and moved the rig over to the Jacoby place in the afternoon. I hadn't been binding for but three maybe four hours and it was time to go home

Greener Pastures

and get ready for dinner. I left the tractor and the binder sitting there in the middle of the field and went home to eat. Now old man Jacoby was pretty heavy into politics and seemed to have gotten more than a few folks upset with some of the things he was up to. That night just after midnight there was a hell of a racket there on our front porch. One of the neighbors was banging on our door, like to beat it down. Seemed that somebody had up and set old man Jacoby's wheat field on fire and we'd better hurry and get our tractor out of there. I pulled on my pants and ran out of the house barefoot. We'd be in a hell of a mess if we were to lose our tractor. I ran barefoot down the road for a quarter of a mile to get to the wheat field, as hard as I could go. The old Farmall had always been pretty good to start and thank God she popped on the second turn of the crank. I shut the compression valves and jumped on the seat. There wasn't any wind, so the fire hadn't overtaken the tractor yet, but it was coming hard. I could feel the heat from the fire on my bare back and the smell of smoke was everywhere. I pulled back the throttle and threw it over into gear. The tractor and I took off straight for the road running over the bundles I had just made. That's probably what saved the tractor was that it was parked in cut wheat where the fire wasn't so hot. I drove right through the fence and into the grader ditch. I didn't slow down until I made the turn into our yard. I got home with only a couple of tears in the canvas from running the fence. After that, I got into the habit of bringing the tractor home with me every evening that it wasn't on our own place.

Things started to look a little better for us that year. I had been able to make some pretty good money hiring out and that fall we even had a little bit of a crop. We didn't pick corn like I had in Northern Iowa but at least we could fill a wagon box by nightfall. That fall though Mom started to feel sick. She wouldn't talk about it she just said that she didn't feel quite right. She should have done a little more looking after herself.

That fall after our corn was picked out, I started picking where I could find work. That's how I come to work for Fred Wenzel for the first time. He was the son of a German Immigrant who farmed over by Eagle. How he came to live down on Steven's Creek, ten miles from Eagle, I don't know. He had nine kids, five girls and four boys. I knew some of the older girls from when I used to be in 4H back in high school before we ever moved to Iowa. I remember well because I think the first time those cows the girls were trying to show had ever seen a halter was when they were drug off to the state fair. They had a hell of a time getting their cows to behave and some of us boys had to help them keep em just from running off let alone get them through the show. Well, two of the older girls were married and moved off now but all four boys were still at home. The two younger ones were still too young to be much good in the field, but the older ones were damned near my age. Fred had

Greener Pastures

a Hell of a time with them boys. Said it was more work than it was worth to get them out in the field to work. Truth was he was just too hard on em. So, I hired on to help him pick corn. I got to know him pretty good. You work three feet away from somebody for three weeks straight and you can't help but to get to know somebody. Turned out that getting to know Fred was a pretty good deal for me. Later on, I spent quite a bit of time either working for Fred or trading work with him. He was also good about letting you borrow and implement or two that you needed if you were working for him. That saved us from having to buy a lot of stuff that you didn't use that often. Which was a big help while we were trying to get back on our feet. The important thing was that Fred got to know I was a good worker. An old, callused farmer like him judged you first by how hard you worked and second by everything else. If you weren't a worker, you weren't worth a Goddamn and He never thought twice about telling you so.

When Fred was picked out, I found my way down to Plattsmouth. There was an old boy down there who had 70-bushel corn. That ain't so hot now but back then we never had all the hybrid corn that we have now, so 70-bushel corn was pretty good. It was damn good considering we were lucky to even get a crop. It was good enough corn and money that for the next four years I took 30 days off and went down to Plattsmouth to pick corn.

Greener Pastures

The next spring, I started to work for Ed Haufman. The Haufman place was just down the road from the Wenzel place, so it wasn't too far from home. He had a quarter section on Havelock Avenue that Steven's Creek cut through. He had one milk cow and Ed did the milking. I did the farming for him. He had two tractors, an old Farmall and a 2236 International. Ed paid me better money than I had ever seen before. For a day's work, I got $2 plus my room and board. I stayed in the farmhouse till about June when I started sleeping in the corncrib because it was just too hot in the old farmhouse. Every day at 4:30 am Ed would call me to breakfast. By golly, if you were going to eat you had to get there before Ed left to go feed the hogs. If you weren't there, He'd throw your breakfast to the hogs and just see what you were going to eat. Dinner was ready at 5 p.m. except during harvest. That was a pretty good deal cause then you had the whole evening for yourself.

Mom still wasn't herself yet, but she kept saying not to worry that it was just something that she was going to have to get over on her own. Besides she had the two girls there to look after the garden and take care of the house for her. That fall I picked corn for Fred Wenzel again before heading down to Plattsmouth. One Saturday night I got up the balls to ask his daughter Mildred out on a date. Fred was just as protective of his girls as he was hard on his boys. He would hardly let one of them out with anybody. Most of the time when the boys would come calling Fred would always say no. I guess I must have been enough of a worker to measure up for him cause he let her go out with me. We didn't date too heavy there that first year, but I kept on calling on her. We'd drive to downtown Lincoln, where we'd park the car down by Gold's department store and watch the cars drive by. Later on, we did a lot of double dating with her older brother Bud, when he started dating my sister Olive. After we sat and watched the cars for a while we might go to a show or sometimes, we just went down to Smith's dairy for an ice cream cone. If we were thirsty, we might head for the Mug or the windmill and get some draft root beer. We didn't dare keep the girls out late, either one of them. Hours had to be kept respectable.

That fall when I came back from picking corn in Plattsmouth, Haufman didn't need me through the winter, so there wasn't any sense in staying there. I wasn't going to be getting paid. Down the road to the south past the Wenzel farm was the Anderson place. Del Anderson had a darned good-sized herd of dairy cattle. He ran enough cows that he kept himself and 2 hire hands busy all year round. One of the boys, Jimmy, was going to move over to Iowa and he was going to be needing another hand. I started working for Del the day after New Year's Day 1938. It was pretty good money. For a day's work, I got $2.50 plus my room and board.

Greener Pastures

Milking cows was steady work, all year round seven days a week. I gave most of what I made to Dad, always had. There were always more bills around the homeplace than he could pay on his own. Every time we moved it took extra money to get started again. Working for Del was just one more way I could help out.

Del Ingerson was a pretty good old cuss. He treated us pretty good. His old wife was another story. Almost all of the milk that we produced was loaded onto Pete Kriner's milk truck and hauled off to Strauss Brothers' dairy. Like everybody else, you only kept back enough for your own use. What he kept back the old woman ran through the separator to get creme for making butter. Then she'd take the skim milk up to the house and put it in the icebox. For as long as I was there that's all we ever had on the table was that damned skim milk. Skim milk wasn't much good to farm boys who all their lives had been used to drinking whole milk, creme, and all. I know it kind of made Del feel bad, but he was too afraid of the old woman to say anything about it. So, he kept a set of tin cups down in the barn. Before we'd close up the milk cans he'd always say, "Drink up boys, she'll never know."

He had a couple of farms that he cultivated. We never hurt for work in the summertime, what with all the milking and the farm work besides. At the same time, there was always a day or two come along here or there when the farm work was a little bit slack. At least it wouldn't hurt too much if it was put off till tomorrow.

93

Greener Pastures

One of the farms was along Highway 34 on the other side of Steven's Creek. To get to it we had to drive the tractor down the highway so we could cross the bridge. Del had the habit of following me over in his old Chevy while I took the tractor. He told the old woman that he did that in case something broke down and he had to go get parts. On the slack days, after lunch, we'd work in the field for a while and then shut down. All the while the old woman would still think we were working in the field. Instead, Del and I would take the old Chevy over to Walton to get a couple of beers. Walton was as small then as it is now, but it did have a grocery store. A family by the name of Straushiem ran the store. It did all right for a small-town market. They didn't really serve beer there as such, but they had it for sale and it damned well got drank there too. There were always a few fellows in between doing something in the afternoon that might be there drinking a beer or two. That's just how afraid he was of the old woman. He had to sneak off when she wouldn't know if he wanted to have a beer. He was a pretty good old cuss, but he was scared to death of that woman. I never did understand why he never stood up to her a little. We couldn't stay around too long; we had to get back in time to start the milking. If we didn't get there by the time the cows started to line up and took off bellowing, then she'd know there was something wrong and would down there wondering what was going on.

Greener Pastures

It was Christmas time again, 1938. I started going over to home more often in between the milking since it was the holidays and all. Mom wasn't getting on too well. She had gotten to the place where she couldn't hide the pain from us anymore. She was sick enough that she could hardly move around the house. Dad took her into Havelock to see a doctor there. The doctor told them that from what he could tell it looked like she had cancer of her female organs. The best thing they could do now was to take her to the hospital and have them removed. A couple of days later we all went into the hospital with Mom for the operation. Things didn't go at all well. When they got her opened up, they found that she was full of cancer. It had spread all over. There wasn't much else that they could do but to close her back up. I'm sure that things might have gone a little differently if she hadn't been so private about it all and had gone to the doctor a little sooner, but those were different times then. You just didn't talk about things like that, not even to your husband.

Dad decided that the best thing to do was to quit farming and move to town so that he could take care of her. He couldn't do the farm work and look after her. One more time the auctioneers would be coming to our place. He called them up and arranged to have a sale the first week of February. This time it was strictly a farm sale. None of the household goods went on the sale but all of the equipment and everything else went. The livestock that was old enough went to market; the young feeders went on the sale. We had four milk cows that went on the sale. Milk cows brought better money on a sale than they did if you took them to market. At market, all you could get was the price of the meat and a good milker was worth more than that.

It kind of hurt me to see the 28 Farmall and the binder go. For the last ten years, I had made a lot of money to help keep the family going with those two machines. Right then though there wasn't anything else to think about. Dad was going to need quite a bit of money to care for Mom.

Dad and Mom never did get moved into town. She died a couple of weeks after the sale. After the funeral, Dad and the girls stayed on the farm till early spring. They knew it wouldn't be right staying there when spring came the Gilmans would have to rent it out to somebody else for farming. Around the end of March, they moved into Havelock. They rented a little house just two houses east of the gas station there at 70th and Havelock Ave. My little brother Pud had just graduated high school and went to work for Gorge Hedges at a dollar a day with room and board. That wasn't too bad for a kid just out of school. Dad and the two girls stayed there in Havelock for a little over a year. My sister Olive had gotten married and moved off to California with her new husband. That left Dad and my younger sister alone in the house. The old house was full of bugs, and they

Greener Pastures

couldn't seem to get rid of them. Dad had been working off and on wherever he could find work, so they didn't have a steady income. They were for the most part just trying to get by.

I had been seeing my girlfriend Mildred pretty frequently, which put me on the Wenzel place quite a bit. Fred Wenzel and a fellow named Goppinger had gotten into running feeder cattle pretty heavy. They were buying enough cows and feeding them out that they had to fence in a lot of new pasture ground, along with keeping all the existing fences up and in good shape. Fred asked me if I thought my dad would come out and work for him making fence and whatnot. He had a hired-hand house that Dad and my sister could live in and plenty of work with the cows.

We moved them out to the Wenzel hired hand house and with them came the bugs. They were in everything, the bedding and all. Soon enough they had overrun the hired hand house. Fred ended up having to have the whole place sprayed to get rid of them. Things worked out all right though for Dad there working for Fred; he stayed working at the Wenzel place till right after Pearl Harbor. My sister Olive sent for him to come and visit her out in California. While he was out there visiting, he found a good job working for the Rheems Manufacturing plant making boilers. He had finally found a place where he could stay on. He worked there at the Rheems plant until his eightieth birthday when he finally decided to

Greener Pastures

retire. When Dad went to California my little sister moved to Boulder, Colorado to stay with my Aunt and Uncle there. I went out to see her once while she was living out there. A little bit later so did my little brother Pud. He was still working for Gorge Hedges when he went out to see her in July. It was just eight months after Pearl Harbor. While he was out there away from the farm, he signed up to join the army. He got to looking around at what there was for him working on the farm and decided that he would be damned if he was going to end up doing that for the rest of his life.

Dad and Olive were out in California, Pud was in the army, Charlie was a Presbyterian minister, my little sister was off at school in Colorado; Mom was gone, and I was the only one left making a living in rural Nebraska doing farm work.

On My Own, for a While and Partnering up

After Mom had died and the family drifted apart, I was left on my own. For the first time in my life, I was completely on my own. I didn't have to worry about supporting the family anymore. Not a care in the world, except for Mildred. I suppose I might have taken off to wandering myself if it hadn't been for her. Besides, I'd been working around Steven's Creek long enough that the town of Walton was starting to feel like a hometown to me. I'd come to know most of the farmers around and their families too. Staying put didn't seem like too bad of an idea for a change.

One thing about being a hired hand and being on your own; you had plenty of time to think. For the first time, I started to think about myself. What was I going to do now that I didn't have to support the family? I knew one thing, I sure as hell didn't want to be a hired hand the rest of my life. I went into Havelock shops and put in for a job with the railroad. I never heard anything from them. I never pushed it either. I didn't want to work in town. So, I never really followed up with checking back. I'd lived on a farm all my life. What in the hell was I going to do in town? Farm work was hard work and all that, but you never had anybody standing over you, telling you what to do. You were free to work at your own pace.

Greener Pastures

As long as you pulled your share, that's all that mattered. I'd always pulled mine and a little more too I suppose.

What I needed was a place of my own. Something that I could work hard at and reap the rewards of my work. Someplace that was mine to run as I pleased. About a mile and a half straight north of the Ingerson place where I was working as a hired hand, there was a widow lady by the name of Mrs. Steward Johnson. She had a quarter section of land that she and her husband used to farm. When her husband died a couple of years ago, she moved into town and rented the farm out. The farmhouse she had rented out to a man by the name of Tom Harris. It had gone downhill a little bit since he had been living there and needed fixing up a bit. He didn't seem to be doing her any good at keeping the place up. The farmland she wasn't having any better luck with. It was rented out to J. R. Reed's hired man Tony Mayer. She wasn't too happy with how he was farming the ground and it wasn't hard to see why. All you had to do was drive by and look over the fields. He had more cockleburs growing than he did corn. It was kind of hard to tell which one he was trying to get to grow. I'd been kicking this idea around in my mind for some time and had been telling Mildred what I thought. It seemed to me that I could do a better job farming the ground than what Mrs. Johnson was getting now. Mildred more than agreed with me.

Greener Pastures

One Sunday afternoon in 1940 after we had been to church Mildred, and I stopped by to see her. After a little bit of small talk, I came around to ask her what she thought about renting the place out to me. It kind of took me by surprise when she said no that she didn't think so. I'd been thinking about it long enough that in my mind I was already moved in. "I got nothing against you Gerald, but I got some plans for the place myself, and I want to rent it out to a family." She said that she was going to have the house remodeled and fixed up. Then when it was respectable again, she wanted to have a family living there. A family that would treat it like a home and keep the place up, like it ought to be kept up.

Well, Mildred and I had talked a little bit about getting married. This just got us to talking a little bit more. What Mildred wanted to do was to go to cosmology school, to learn to fix hair. The only trouble was that when she had told her dad, Fred, about what she wanted to do he had said no, and no was no. None of the girls had ever dared to cross him. They knew better. If the boys dared cross the old man, all hell broke loose on them. It was his way or no way. She was trapped. The only way she was going to get out from under him and live her own life was when she got married. For Christmas of 1940, I gave her a ring. I never really proposed, I just up and gave her a ring. In January we stopped in to see Mrs. Johnson again and tell her what our plans were.

Greener Pastures

The fact that we were going to get married changed things enough for her I guess. She told us that we could have the place, seeing as how we were going to get married and start raising a family on the place. She promised to get the place remodeled and have it ready for us to move into come spring.

Fred and Ethel, Mildred's Dad and Mom, didn't seem to think too much of the Idea though. They were dead set against it. I was eight years older than Mildred and for some reason that just didn't set well. I don't think Ethel wanted any of the girls to get married. She told them that the only thing they were going to know if they got married was having babies, taking care of kids, and doing housework. I don't blame her any. After all, she had had nine of them. Not to mention that she was married to Fred who was about as demanding a man as you could ask for. Just like when he decided it was time that he needed a shave, she had to drop whatever she was doing and shave him. He never shaved himself. That was her job and when he needed a shave, she had to do it. Such had been her life.

There had been something else come up that didn't help me any. It was something that had happened a while back. I think that in a way Fred still held the incident that happened in the barn against me. Earlier that fall I was down in the barn with some of Fred's boys playing basketball. The game got a little competitive and I was never one to back away from a challenge, especially

Greener Pastures

when it came to baseball or basketball. The older boys and I were playing at it pretty hard, and I ended up tripping Marion, one of the little brothers. He wasn't much more than a little snot then and had gotten underfoot. I pretty well knocked him down. When I reached down to pick him up his older brother Bud, who was a bit of a hot head, seemed to think I had done it on purpose and came at me with fists flying. Hell, I had no choice but to defend myself. I had to hit him enough times that he finally kept from coming back at me. I probably should have gone ahead and cleaned his plow, but I had never been raised to fight. That was one thing that my dad had always been against was fighting. He had always told us that you never proved nothing by fighting. So, I picked up my coat and left.

I don't know what the boys told Fred about what had happened down at the barn, or why Bud had his face all bloodied up, but from then on nobody had any use for me around the Wenzel place. Except of course Mildred. She was still with me. We wouldn't be double dating with her brother Bud though.

There wasn't any money to be had for a big wedding and we were half afraid that Fred would try and stop it, so we decided against that. We decided that the best thing was to go out of town and get married. We drove up to the courthouse in Omaha and were married by the judge there. That way there wasn't anything that Fred could do about it. We never let on though that we had gotten married. I kept working at the Ingerson place and Mildred stayed at home. We weren't going to tell anyone until the house was ready for us. For all anybody knew were still just dating. We bought a table and chairs and some of the other things that we knew we were going to need and kept them over at Fred's house. We got along just fine with our little charade till Ethel noticed that her daughter was starting to show with child. She didn't say anything to her right off though she waited till Fred came home to jump her about it. I'm glad I wasn't there to hear what all was said about me. Things were hot enough for Mildred though. She finally had to go and get out the marriage certificate to prove it to them. Thank goodness the house was ready to move into. It sure took Fred a while to get used to it. He came around though. One day he showed up at our place with a pregnant sow and a dozen chicks from Hill Hatchery. That may not sound like much of a wedding gift, but that was a hell of a gift to a farmer. A pregnant sow would get you started raising hogs. That meant cash money and meat on the table. Chickens meant eggs. Eggs to eat and eggs that you could sell in town. The sow gave us trouble, she kept getting out and running back to Fred's. It wasn't until she had the litter that she finally stayed put.

I needed a little more help to get started farming on my own. I'd worked all my life, but everything had always gone to the family and every bit of that went on the sale.

Greener Pastures

I got a Farm Security loan to help me get started. With the loan, I bought four milk cows and a team of horses. It wasn't much but it would get us started. In the morning I'd milk our four cows and then head to Del Ingerson's and milk his too. When it came time to do the spring planting, I got both my farming done and his too. It made for some pretty long hard days. Dawn to dusk and then some. Seemed like that was what farming on my own was going to be like for a good long while.

We had a decent place to live though. Mrs. Johnson had put in a brand-new copper-clad wood-burning cook stove and an oil burner for heat. The house had beautiful oak wooden floors. They weren't the old splinted-out boards that most of the old farmhouses had. It was a better house than I'd lived in for quite a while.

I borrowed a disk and a lister from my father-in-law Fred, to get the crops in with. Come the middle of July though Mom was ready to have our baby. We went into Bryan Hospital to have her delivered. She was there for ten days. It cost $75. That was the whole bill for everything, except for Old Doc Taylor who delivered her; he cost another $25. We named her Bonnie. She was a baby girl born on July 11, 1941.

The Johnson place had some good farmland. It had some good grassland too. The north end of the place was native prairie grass. Some of it I run the cows on and the rest I let grow to cut for hay. Once we had all the crops in, I was starting to think about cutting hay. Out of the blue one day, my father-in-law Fred shows up. He came in as if nothing had ever happened between us and asked me if I would help him get his hay in. He said if I would come down and help him bale his hay then he'd come up and help me get mine in. Just like that everything was patched up. I never found out why till much later, but I guess he found out what really happened down at the barn that day. From then on things couldn't have been better between us. Old Fred did everything he could to help us make it. Or at least what he thought we ought to do.

So, I went down with him to tie wire. He and old Ed Weddingcamp and I had the job of running the baler. It was long hard work tying bales and Old Ed Weddingcamp didn't make it any shorter. Ed was Fred's neighbor down the road to the south, just past the Ingerson's. Those two, Fred and Ed were two peas in a pod. They'd been evolved in more adventures than the Hardy boys. Together they'd done everything from sawing lumber to hitching rides to Montana in a box car. While I tied, they took turns pitching hay into the baler. Fred was pretty good. If I'd call out for half or three-quarters of a fork to finish off a bale, that's exactly what I would get, Ed was a different story. If I'd call for half a bale he'd pitch in the biggest fork yet, then I'd have to splice the wires. The wires were precut to length and if the bale got too big you had to splice a short piece onto the end. After we got Fred's hay put up, he came and helped me get mine in. Mildred started going down to see her mom again and things were the way they should be.

In the mornings I'd put the milk cans in the horse tank to keep them cool until Pete Kriner came along to pick them up and I'd go down to the Ingerson's to milk. When Pete came along to pick up the milk Mildred would ride with him down to her mom's place with the baby. Mildred's little brother and sister, Gene, and Florence, were young enough that our little girl Bonnie was just like a little sister to them. When it came time to harvest our wheat, her mom kept the baby so that Mildred could drive the tractor and I could run the binder.

That first year of farming we did okay. We made enough money to buy a John Deere Model "D" tractor and an old 1936 model "B" Ford. The damned old thing used so much oil that it took two quarts to drive to town and back. I used the old dirty oil out of the tractor in it cause it used so much. That's what we drove through, during the war.

We stayed on at the Johnson place till after the war. Things were going pretty good for us there. Being we were so close I started doing more and more for old Fred. He was getting on in years, but he still worked like he was a twenty-year-old. I helped him at harvest time getting the crop cut. He had a pretty good-sized crew working during the harvest and I was part of it. Fred would bring the crew up to our place and in one day we'd have it cleaned out and move on to the next.

Goppinger was still doing business around these parts. He and Fred were about the same age. They had thrown in with each other a time or two and Fred and he were pretty thick together. Goppinger was a fairly intelligent fellow, he had himself quite a bit of money built up from speculating and the like too. Not that old Fred was any dummy, but he never had any money for speculating. Goppinger, he'd go up into South Dakota and buy these white face feeder calves and drive them to the train yard so they could be shipped down to Walton. Fred and the boys would drive them home and feed them out for a year. When the market was right they'd sell them for slaughter and they'd split the profit over what Goppinger had paid for them. Goppinger provided the money and Fred provided the work. It was a pretty good deal for both of them.

Worked out good enough that both Goppinger and old Fred were able to buy a few quarter sections of land around the county. The more land they had the more cattle they could feed out. It got so Fred couldn't handle it all. Not to mention the boys were getting married off. Fred would help them get started, he'd set them up on one of Goppinger's farms feeding out cattle. Goppinger had a big farm south of Walton, that Fred seemed to think that we needed to move to. It meant more work but that also meant more money. We'd had ourselves

Greener Pastures

another little girl, Evelyn, in 1944 so a little extra money wouldn't hurt a thing. In 1945 we moved south of Walton and started running white face cows for old Goppinger. Those were good years. The late forties were probably the best years there ever was for farming. If you couldn't make it then, you probably weren't going to.

It was there that the girls started to school. They started off going to a little country school a couple of miles to the south. If it was good weather, they'd walk down. Otherwise, I'd drive them to school. Except if it rained. If it had just rained hard, we lived on a mud road and the road would have to dry a little before we'd go anywhere.

Now that we lived farther away from Fred's we had to have a better car. We bought a new Chevrolet sedan after the war was over and they started making cars again. Fred had cows all over the county and I spent a lot of time driving to his place or to one of the farms he was working.

Fred was a hard-driving son of a buck to work for. He expected you to work as hard as he did. You did it his way and that was that. The older he got the more set in his ways he became. Hell, it wasn't a whole lot different than it had been working for my old man so we got along fine. Fred's boys didn't see it that way. They were just about as stubborn and set in their ways as he was. When Fred got into it with one of the kids all Hell broke loose.

Greener Pastures

They couldn't both be right, but they both damned sure insisted they were.

Seemed like he was the hardest on the two younger boys. Marion got married to a girl from down around Elmwood and moved out. That left Gene the littlest one at home. All the other kids were married except for Florence, the youngest girl, and Bud, the oldest boy. If Fred wasn't dealing out punishment to Gene, Bud was. He was every bit as hard on the boy as his dad was. Things got a bit hard on the boy.

Mildred and I had a good-sized chicken house that she collected eggs from and took them into town to sell. Eggs didn't bring in that much, but it was spending money and could help out with paying for other groceries that you needed. Mildred had the habit of stopping by her folks' house on her way into town to sell the eggs. One day Gene was waiting for her to come and take him into town. He was all worked up about something and chomping at the bit to get into town. He was in such a toot that he wanted to drive. He had to get somewhere before they closed up. They took off flying down the road toward town. Just past 70th Street, they hit a good hump in the road and the eggs that were sitting on the back seat went flying. He'd broke all but a dozen of the eggs. Mildred started crying cause now the grocery money was lost and what was she supposed to do? Gene was still all worked up though. He was off to see the Marine recruiters. He was more or less running away from home. Hell, he was only 16 years old. He had to lie about his age. The Korean War was going on and they needed recruits, so they were glad to look the other way about his being underage.

It was in 1950 when my boy Bruce was born. When Bonnie was born, Mom wanted a girl, and I guess I didn't care either way. But by golly when Bruce was born, I was like to bust my buttons. Drove all over the county handing out cigars like a damned fool, I did. Three kids were enough for us. We didn't have any more after Bruce. Not that they wouldn't have been welcome if they had come along.

That winter in 1951 we had a hell of a snowstorm. It started to snow in the morning, and it didn't let off. I was up at Fred's place working and just about didn't get home with the Chevy. I left Fred's early, right after dinner, and headed for home. It snowed so hard I couldn't hardly see the road. It was all that I could do to get home. I got stuck on the road just before I got home and had to walk the rest of the way through the snow. I was lucky that I made it home at all, and didn't get lost in the swirling snow. When I got in the door Mom was about half crazy about the girls. They hadn't come home from school, and we had no idea if they were alive or frozen. We couldn't go looking for them, I couldn't even risk trying to make it to the barn and back. We just had to hope they were safe somewhere. The storm kept up

Greener Pastures

until the next day. There wasn't anything you could do but to stay inside. I couldn't even worry after the cattle.

Two days later I rode the horse over through the drifts to the schoolhouse to see if anybody knew anything about the kids and where they were. I found them over to Augusta Bethune's. She lived just across from the school and the girls had stayed there. I put them up on the horse with me one in front and the other behind. Together we rode through the drifts back home. After two days of not knowing if they were alive or dead, it was good to have them home again.

We had mud roads clear up until my boy Bruce started school. I kept the old touring car around for if it started to rain and I had to get the girls home from school. It had skinny tires and could churn through mud that the Chevy couldn't even think of getting through. Just because it could make it down a mud road, I kept it in the back of the corn crib and kept it in good enough shape to use now and then. The Chevy was a better car, but the old Ford was the only thing short of a tractor that could get down the mud road. Once they brought gravel down the road, I let the old car go to hell.

Goppinger was a pretty good landlord. By 1952 a lot of the county had electricity. When Norris Public Power ran the line down the road a half a mile to the north Goppinger got them to run a line down to the house. Electricity changes almost everything. Once we had it

Greener Pastures

Goppinger put us in an electric well pump and brought water into the house. He put us in an indoor bathroom. That was a pretty big step having plumbing in the house. We still had the same cook stove though. Mom kept cooking with corn cobs and cordwood for a good spell longer. I bought her an electric washing machine though. It was a wringer type. Up until then, we had to drag the clothes out to the wash house, heat the water, and belt up the gasoline engine to the washing machine. Things were getting easier on the farm.

Pull combines had come out doing away with binders and thrashers. Corn pickers meant that you didn't have to pick corn by hand anymore. What it meant was that you could farm more ground with less help. I rented out another small farm nearby and still kept on helping Fred with his work as I could. I helped Fred the most at harvest time. I helped him get his crops in and then he helped me with getting mine in. Fred had an old grain truck so when we picked corn, we set up a sheller right there in the field. We'd shell it out right in the field and haul it into Walton without the cobs. You could haul a lot more corn without the cobs.

Fred's second oldest boy, Oliver, had come back from the service. The first thing he did when he got back was to get Fred to go into the Mercury dealer and buy a brand new shiny blue Mercury sedan. That was the first wide tired car that Fred had ever had. He was still driving an old Model "A" Ford. Fred used to like to drive that car

Greener Pastures

up to the north place to check on the cattle. I went along with him plenty of times in the winter when there wasn't that much else to do. We usually went in the afternoon after lunch was out of the way. We took Cornhusker Highway out to 14th Street and then headed north out to where the cattle were pastured. There were a couple of Bars that we drove by along the highway. Fred almost always got a little thirsty during the trip and we'd stop off and have a few beers. I'd half to remind him a few times of what we were supposed to be doing or we might not have ever got out to check on those cows. Come to think about it I think those cows got checked on a whole lot more than they needed to be. On the way home He'd be hankering to stop off again. Most of the time I could keep him heading home and we could still make it home in time for supper.

Fred liked his beer and he liked to work hard. But he didn't believe in mixing the two. Work was work and you'd better be able to do more than your share if you were going to be around Fred. Time was though when he was first married, he used to like to drive the team into Eagle and hoist a few too many in the Eagle bar. It didn't matter so much back then. All you had to do was crawl into the back of the wagon and the team would take the wagon back home. Good thing he grew out of that foolishness by the time that cars come around. The old model "A" Ford just couldn't find its way home like

Greener Pastures

the team could. The new Mercury didn't do any better job either.

Oliver and Fred drove the Blue Mercury out north one day to harvest corn. Harvesting corn had changed a bit now that corn pickers had come along. It took a lot less time to pick a wagon full of corn. You could pick a wagon full of corn faster than you could haul it home so most of the farmers started shelling the corn in the field if they were picking any distance from where they were going to store it. The corn shellers were left over from the horsepower days. The only difference was that now they were belted up to a tractor instead of a jackshaft. You still had to shovel the corn in by hand. They'd left early in the morning to get a good day's work in picking and shelling. Oliver was out in the field running the corn picker and Fred was back up by the road shoveling ears into the sheller. The first corn pickers did a decent enough job, but they left a few husks on the ears. You had to clean these out of the sheller, or it would get clogged. Fred reached down into the sheller to pull some husks out of the way and his cotton work glove got caught in the bevel gears. Before he could get his hand pulled out of the sheller it had taken three fingers off his right hand. He got a really weak feeling and had to sit down on the ground. Oliver was still out in the field running the corn picker. There wasn't any good for him to shout cause Oliver couldn't hear him over the noise the machinery made. It was probably half an hour before Oliver came back and found him barely conscious and ready to pass out. He picked him up and carried him to the Mercury and they went flying down to the neighbors. Oliver ran in just long enough to tell them to call the police and have an escort ready at the edge of town to take them to the hospital. With Fred about ready to go into shock Oliver buried the pedal into the floorboards and the Mercury roared off for town. They met the police escort at the edge of town which probably did more to slow them down than anything. But maybe it was for the best or they might have been doing eighty down 48th Street headed for Bryan Hospital.

Fred made it through alright, but he didn't have much of a right hand left. It wasn't much good for any of the kind of work he was used to doing. The accident made an old man out of him in a hurry.

It wasn't too long after his hand got torn up that Goppenger decided that the economics of buying feeder cattle wasn't going to keep paying off as it had. He just couldn't get feeder cattle cheap enough. Fred came up with the idea that we ought to let the pastures go to seed and see if we could make some money selling brome grass seed. The government had been buying a lot of brome grass for reconstruction projects over in Europe, fixing up some of the land that had been torn up from the war and all. That had driven the price of brome seed to a false high and it was selling for a lot more than it otherwise would have been.

Greener Pastures

We bought fertilizer for the pastures, and it looked like we were going to have a pretty good crop going. Fred started to look around for where the best place would be to market the seed. We had found a few places that were looking to take a bid on brome. The best one was from a place down in Kansas. They were offering to pay 21 cents a bushel, but we were going to have to pay to have it freighted down. This Kansas outfit seemed to want it pretty bad. They were willing to take all that we had. Somehow or other Griswold's Seed out of Lincoln got wind of it and they sent their buyer out to see me. I told them what they'd half to beat if they wanted in on it and they'd have to take it all, what I had and what Fred had. He guaranteed me that they would take all that we had for 22 cents a bushel. I went inside to call Fred just to make sure that he was in agreement, which he was. I came back out and told the fellow from Griswold's Seed "Mister looks like you got yourself a deal".

The brome turned out to be better than even we had expected. Fred went and bought a new combine to cut it all with so that we would have two machines. Good thing he did too. We had gotten all of his cut and had the machines down to my place when it started to look like it was going to rain. We started cutting and didn't stop until the rain and the wind came up, so we had to. We had gotten all but about 5 acres cut before we had to quit. The rain and the wind whipped the grass so hard that by the time the sun came out again, we could finish cutting. What was left didn't hardly make it worth

Greener Pastures

cutting. The seed had all shaken out since it was heavy with rain. Didn't matter much though, we still had us one hell of a crop. Those fellows from Griswold's held up their end of the bargain. They took it all at 22 cents. I know darned well they wished they hadn't had to take so much, and I think in the end they had a hard time moving so much. For us, it paid for the new combine Fred had bought and went a long way toward fixing things up on the farms we had.

Those last few years of farming had been pretty good for all of us. Fred was getting on in years and the boys were having to take over and do more and more of the work. His wife Ethel had a stroke and before she could recover fully from it another one took her away from him. About a year later Fred died from a heart attack. I didn't do a whole lot better. I started to have problems with an ulcer. One day I was out riding the tractor across the field to go check on the cattle when every bump I hit started to shoot pain through my abdomen. What started out like a green apple bellyache turned into a bleeding ulcer. It was all I could do to get to help. That sure took the wind out of my sails. All the neighbors and family had to pitch in and do the farm work for us. My wife Mildred was convinced that it was all the hard work we did that caused it and if I kept it up it was going to kill me. She talked me into giving up the fight and trying to make it out on the farm anymore. I wasn't in any shape to argue with her. We had a sale and moved into

Bethany. I had spent almost a lifetime on the farm. What time was left for me I'd finish out in town. I worked as a cabinet maker for a few years. Then I got on with the grounds department at the university's east campus. It was good to work with tractors and machinery again. I got to work outside again. The only bad thing about being a groundskeeper on the campus is that when it snows, and the weather is bad, you have to get out and work to clean the streets and walks.

I spent the rest of my working days, that is the ones for pay, with the University. Once I retired, I went back to helping my brother-in-law with his farm work. There were a lot of stories that could be told about the Ag college and the farming that I did afterward, but those will have to be told another time.

ABOUT THE AUTHOR

Herbert Sack is a Native of the State of Nebraska and a graduate of the University of Nebraska where he studied creative writing. He has lived an adventurous life having traveled extensively throughout Mexico, and Central and South America. He speaks Spanish fluently. His bucket list is very short. "There is very little that I want to do that I haven't already done." He enjoys bike riding, kayaking, and rhythm guitar. His songs, some originals, can be found on his YouTube site.

OTHER WORKS BY HERBERT SACK

These works are currently available by contacting the author by email at herbertsack56@gmail.com

The Return of the Iguana

Short Stories from a Creative Mind

Historias de una Mente Creativa

The Passport Murders

Printed in Dunstable, United Kingdom